W9-ANG-089

"Dancey uses tender, raw honesty to trudge through her mountain of despair, all the while building a stairway to the mountain of hope that only our God can provide."

Kelly Prisby, sister in Christ

"Through Karen's story, you will see an inside glimpse into God's sovereignty and love. God gave Karen an extreme soul makeover experience. He delivered her and turned sorrow and pain into joy and hope."

Maryann Gilliam, recipient of a home
built by ABC's hit show
[Extreme Makeover: Home Edition]

MOUNTAIN OF
HOPE

KAREN DANCEY

WESTBOW
P R E S S
A DIVISION OF THOMAS NELSON

WestBow Press books may be ordered through booksellers or by contacting:

WestBow Press
A Division of Thomas Nelson
1663 Liberty Drive
Bloomington, IN 47403
www.westbowpress.com
1-(866) 928-1240

Because of the dynamic nature of the Internet, any web addresses or
links contained in this book may have changed since publication and
may no longer be valid. The views expressed in this work are solely those
of the author and do not necessarily reflect the views of the publisher,
and the publisher hereby disclaims any responsibility for them.

Certain stock imagery © Thinkstock.
Any people depicted in stock imagery provided by Thinkstock are models,
and such images are being used for illustrative purposes only.

Scripture quotations are taken from the *Concordia Self Study Bible*.
Saint Louis: Concordia Publishing House, 1986 Using the New
International Version. 1973. Editor Robert G. Hoetber

ISBN: 978-1-4497-1646-2 (e)
ISBN: 978-1-4497-1647-9 (sc)
ISBN: 978-1-4497-1648-6 (hc)

Library of Congress Control Number: 2011928527

Printed in the United States of America

WestBow Press rev. date: 5/25/2011

To Eric, Jeremy, and Keith
I am honored and so very glad that
God chose me to be your mom.

To Jessica, Derek, Caitlin, Angela, Kate, and Emma
I am humbled that your parents chose
me to be your godmother.

To Dorothy Matzinger
Juliann Rose
Denise Nicholson
Melinda Finkel
Judy Hafner
Kelly Davenport
Here is hope for the journey.

In Loving Memory
Matthew Eric Matzinger
Rex Alan Matzinger
Nancy Ruth Lederer
I wasn't ready to say good-bye.

CONTENTS

CHAPTER 1

A PASTOR'S HOME OF HOPE

It wasn't a typical Father's Day gift. The following heartfelt words were written with love and gratitude to my dad, Pastor E. Paul Burow.

And how ironic that perhaps the most treasured memory of all took place on the most tragic day of all. I collapsed into my dad's arms upon hearing the shocking news that my husband of almost fourteen years was dead. All of a sudden I was a widow and single mother to three very young boys with no home to call my own. The special, bittersweet memory I will cherish forever is the comforting, providing words of my father: "Don't worry, Karen. I will take care of you." In that single moment, I wanted to go from a thirty-six-year-old daughter to a six-year-old daughter. I longed for my childhood days when life was so simple and happy and carefree. As the numbness wore off and reality sank in, I knew that this was a wound much too deep for my dad to fix.

Back when I was six years old, my human dad could do no wrong. In Sunday school class one day, the teacher was explaining to us how everyone sins and needs God's forgiveness. I was very upset with her for saying that everyone sins. With great

1

determination and confidence I yelled, "My dad does not sin! He is a pastor."

I am much older and wiser now and I realize that my dad is not perfect but I still consider him one of the best dads around. Countless times throughout my childhood and young adulthood I was asked, "What is it like having a dad who is a pastor?" He was my dad and I loved and respected him very much. He taught us more by living out his faith than what we could have learned in a thousand sermons. Thankfully he did not preach to us all day but he did demonstrate many practical and spiritual lessons through his daily behavior.

Often the practical and spiritual lessons intertwined. He had a great sense of humor and was always making us laugh. Laughter could be especially heard at the dinner table. It was my favorite time of the day because the entire family was together. Dad, Mom, Jennifer, Peter, Sarah (my siblings), and I would all take turns talking about our day. We spent more time laughing than we did talking.

Another lesson he taught me was how to enjoy the moment. Dad's enthusiasm was contagious on snow days. He would come running into our room. "Girls, look out the window and see all the snow! There is no school today." He was always eager to take us sledding.

My mom would say, "Precious Paulie, it is not safe to drive on the roads today."

He replied, "Oh, Peggy, it will be fun. Come with us." And off we all went to enjoy an afternoon of sledding.

A third lesson was time management. Dad would tell us that there was a time to work and a time to play. I laugh when I hear people ask, "Do pastors only work on Sunday mornings?" There were plenty of times when I wished my dad had been home more.

He worked at church all day, came home to eat dinner, and then went back to church for meetings or to counsel people. There was some flexibility in his schedule, though, and he took the time to teach me the basic skills of basketball and softball. He was thrilled for me when I made both teams and he was able to come to most of my games.

With my dad's busy work schedule, it was nice having my mom at home. Mom was the one that kept the household running smoothly. She is still known for always having a smile on her face. She had a heart to serve her family and those in need. She lived out her faith in the way she talked and in her every day actions. During an interview I had in college I was asked to name someone I admire. I said "My mother."

My parents loved each other very much. They would often hug and kiss in the kitchen. I would say, "Do you have to keep doing that in front of me?" They would tell me what a blessing it was that I had parents who showed affection. They knew how to have fun together. They played tennis together, joined the church bowling league, played bridge, and took walks together. I never had to live with the fear that my parents would ever divorce. Moreover, I knew I was loved and accepted and no matter how rotten a day I had at school, I could come home to a safe, loving, fun place. What a blessing!

Another blessing was having my dad as one of my confirmation teachers. Confirmation in the Lutheran church meant that I was publicly confirming my baptism. I spoke from my heart that I accepted Jesus Christ as my Lord and Savior. My dad helped me choose my confirmation verse which was John 8:12: *Jesus says, "I am the light of the world. Whoever follows me will never walk in darkness, but will have the light of life."* To me, this meant that Jesus promised to be my light. Jesus would help me choose good over evil (light over darkness). Living in darkness meant living a life apart from God and there is no hope in that. I wanted hope. I wanted the joy and peace that I saw in my parents' lives. Their lives were full of peace, goodness, truth, and hope. In other words, they reflected the light of Jesus and that is how I wanted to live my life.

On the lighter side of confirmation, we were able to enjoy some social activities. My dad was in charge of a bowling outing with the confirmands. I offered to help organize the teams so that I could put my best friend, Sue, on my team. I had a big crush on one of the guys so I made sure he was on my team as well. He was tall, dark, and handsome and I was in LOVE. Little did I know at the time that he would be my future husband.

His name was J. F. Matt Matzinger. We went to different schools and only saw each other on Sunday mornings. Matt's family always sat in the same spot at church so I would sit right in front of him so he could look at me all during church and fall in love with me. As soon as the school year ended, Matt and his parents moved four hours away, so we lost touch all during high school.

As a teenager, I realized that being a pastor's daughter comes with some important responsibilities. I did not take that responsibility seriously when I answered the phone late one Saturday night. A lady asked for my dad and I told her he wasn't home yet because I didn't think he was. She told me that her husband had just died. My dad WAS home and asked me what the phone call was about. I lied and said wrong number because I thought I would get in trouble for not checking to see if my dad was home.

The next morning in church, my dad prayed for healing for this person. When my dad arrived home after the Sunday service, he was fuming with me. "How could you not tell me that someone had died? Do you know how stupid I felt praying for that person? Not only that, but I had to apologize to the widow. You are never allowed to answer the phone again!" Looking back, I think my dad was way too easy on me.

I can now see my lack of maturity and my lack of sympathy for this widow. I treated her phone call carelessly and was more concerned with staying out of trouble than with her heartbreaking situation. I did not have a clue as to the enormity of her loss. My life was happy and sheltered. I had no personal experience with tragedy during my childhood days.

With the responsibilities also came aggravations. My high school religion teacher would call on me when nobody raised their hand. He assumed I knew all the answers because my dad was a pastor. My answer was always "I don't know" whether I knew the answer or not. I didn't want the other students to think that I was a "Bible know-it-all," which I definitely was not. The teacher finally quit calling on me after my dad had a talk with him.

The majority of my high school social life revolved around the church youth group. My parents did not force this on me. I chose to be active in the group because it was fun. During my junior year I dated a boy from youth group. He was younger than me and it was a very innocent relationship. When he broke up with me, I was crushed.

My dad was a great counselor. I asked him to take a walk with me so I could express my sadness over my break up. My dad started out by saying, *"Don't worry, Karen. There are other fish in the sea. But seriously, I am sorry. I know you are hurting. It is tough being sixteen with a broken heart. You are a precious child of God and someday, God-willing, you will meet a man who fits into God's purpose for your life. You will go through life with disappointments, but God will never disappoint you. You may not like your circumstances, but God will remain your steady Rock. Think of God as your first love and as your last love. With God there is always hope. God will never leave you. God will never abandon you. God will never break up with you. I love you, Karen, and I am very proud of you. If boys can't see what a blessing you are, then they don't deserve to date you. Look on the bright side. Now you have more free time to stay home and play ping-pong with us."* My dad always tried to end conversations with humor.

I spent many Saturday nights babysitting my younger brother and sister, Peter and Sarah, because my parents were invited to several weddings. There were times when my older sister Jennifer and I would both be home babysitting. Although Jennifer was two years older than me, I considered us equally in charge. The following babysitting incident is a favorite among our family. Jennifer was the worrier in the family.

Around eleven o'clock on a snowy winter night, Jennifer, who was eighteen at the time, kept hearing noises. She was convinced someone was breaking into our house. I was sixteen and told her she was being paranoid and that she needed to calm down. I heard the noise but it sounded like it was outside. Jennifer couldn't take it any longer and she called the police. Jennifer and I had to walk downstairs together to unlock the back door. I have to admit that I was starting to feel scared at this point. When we opened the door we realized that one of the police officers went to our church and knew our family.

The policemen asked who was all in the house. We told them we were babysitting our younger brother and sister. They asked if anyone was in the basement. We said "No". One of the officers went downstairs and saw someone. They aimed their flashlight at the face and yelled, "This is the police! Put your hands in the air."

My half asleep brother, Peter, who was ten years old, sat up in bed and said "I didn't do it!" In all the nervousness of the evening, we had forgotten that Peter recently moved to the bedroom in the basement. It turns out the noise we heard was the snowplow bumping into the curb. Sarah was eight and had remained asleep through the entire embarrassing event.

Family stories are great to carry down from generation to generation. I remember sitting on my Grandma Burow's front porch eating ice cream cones and visiting with her. I loved hearing stories from her childhood and stories about my dad. My grandmother had a deep faith and she leaned on God's strength often. She shared the difficulties of caring for my dad when he was six years old and had polio. She never lost hope because she had God to give her the daily strength she needed. My dad recently wrote about his battle with polio.

"My Doctor Israel thought that I picked up the polio virus while swimming in a creek at our church picnic in August of 1944. By September of that year I was completely paralyzed from the waist down. In the 1940's

many victims of polio were in iron lungs and for those who were fortunate to survive most had serious side effects and a shortened life span. There were so many cases of polio in the Buffalo, New York area that the victims were put in a converted warehouse that was turned into the Children's Hospital annex. I only spent ten days at this make shift hospital and woke up every night to the cries and screams of nearly 100 children in this place.

Dr. Israel encouraged my parents to keep me at home and to use the "Sister Kenney" method for my treatment. This meant that my mother and a nurse had to put hot packs on my legs and back three times a day plus give me two very hot baths. The flannel packs were so hot that I cried because they burned my skin. Dr. Israel was a very caring physician who made regular house calls to encourage us and monitor my care. He had lost his own son to polio and he took me on as his special patient. One day he told my mother that he was confident that I would recover and that her love and our faith in the Lord were a big part of the healing process.

I remember the day months later when I went to his office and for the first time since early September I was able to move my toes. I can still hear the cheers of my parents and my doctor and his staff. I know that this was truly the day that the Lord had made. To this day I thank my God for HIS gracious healing. Years later when people asked me why I went into the ministry I would tell them because I felt that God had delivered me from this terrible disease so that I could serve His people with the Good News of Jesus. The only side effects that I have experienced throughout the years are a weakened back and a weird sense of humor."

My dad recently celebrated his seventy-second birthday and is still working in ministry. My mom's parents are ninety-one-years-old and I am blessed to still have them in my life. They have always been an inspiration to me as well. Serving others came naturally to them. Their life together has been richly blessed. They often say, "Karen, always give to God first. Trust that God will take care of you. God must be first in your life."

What a rich heritage of faith I had been given. Nevertheless, I knew I couldn't rely on my parents' faith or my grandparents' faith. I had to make my own decision about Jesus. I wanted Jesus but I hadn't fully surrendered my life to Him.

I was making big decisions on my own without asking for God's input. I had always planned to go to college after high school graduation. My grades were average but I had scored low on my college entrance exams. My guidance counselor looked at my test score and told me not to bother applying to colleges because I wouldn't get in. She did not suggest I retake the test. She did not offer any hope. She apparently had no idea how devastating those words were to me.

My parents encouraged me to go to a community college. Believing I was not fit for college, I enrolled in a business school instead. This was the fall of 1987. The classes were easy for me and I enjoyed having the reputation as the smart student by both the students and faculty alike. This success gave me the confidence I needed to eventually go to college and graduate with honors.

On New Year's Eve 1987, my best friend, Sue, was home from college and we were hanging out at her house. We were bored and decided to call Matt. Matt was the tall, dark, and handsome boy I had a crush on in confirmation class. I was too shy to call so I made Sue call him. At this point in time, Matt lived four hours away but we were hoping he was in the area visiting his sister, Kathleen. Kathleen said he had gone back home but that he would be driving back down state in a couple of weeks. She asked, "Who is calling?"

Sue looked at me and answered, "This is Karen Burow."

To which I responded, "Sue! I can't believe you just said that!"

CHAPTER 2

HOPING FOR A DATE

A few weeks later Matt was back in town visiting his sister. Our telephone rang. This was long before caller ID so I casually picked up the phone and said, "Hello."

"Hey Karen, this is Matt. I heard that you called." I do not remember if I told him it was Sue that had made the original phone call. All I remember is that I was so nervous and so excited all at the same time.

He was telling me that he and a friend were in the area for a training seminar. They were preparing to volunteer at a crisis center. Matt asked, "Would you like to have lunch on Sunday with my friend and me at Pizza Hut?"

I managed to come down from cloud nine and calmly say, "Sure." I hung up the phone and screamed. My family came running and asked, "What's wrong Karen?"

I replied, "I have a date with Matt!" I do not know if it was technically a date because he did have a friend with him, but I like to think of it as our first date.

Matt was even cuter than I remembered. Lunch went by much too fast and I was wondering if or when I would get to see him again. As lunch was ending Matt asked for my phone number and address. "YES!" I silently screamed. We said our good-byes and promised to write. The letters started streaming in. We may not have had the convenience of e-mail, but we did have the romance of savoring each hand-written letter and sealing the envelopes with a kiss.

Matt was back in town that Easter weekend and we were able to spend some quality time together. We walked around downtown Rochester, Michigan and strolled through the park. Matt and I watched a movie at his sister's house and his niece and nephew kept spying on us. Towards the end of the movie, Matt kissed me. I was in heaven. The following day we played Pictionary and Trivial Pursuit with his family. I loved playing the games and getting to know his family. I fell in love with all of them. On Easter Sunday, my mom agreed to let Matt eat dinner with us.

I was a bit nervous as the dynamics in my family were different from his. Matt was the youngest of five children. His four sisters were quite a bit older than him. My family was younger and I was afraid Matt would think my family was immature. His family conversations sounded more intellectual whereas my family had more light-hearted conversations around the dinner table. To my surprise, Matt felt at ease around my family and enjoyed wrestling and teasing my younger siblings. Matt also got along well with my older sister Jennifer and answered all of her questions.

Matt grew up in Romeo, Michigan with his parents and four older sisters. His sisters were cheerleaders and gymnasts with a whole lot of enthusiasm. Matt shared stories of how they would babysit him and use him in their gymnastic stunts. Due to the age gap, Matt was raised like an only child. By the time Matt was eight years old, all four sisters were out of the house. The twins, Joanna and Carolyn, were ten years older than Matt. Ellen Marie was twelve years older, and Kathleen was fifteen years his senior.

Matt was tall, thin and looked like a basketball player. However, he chose to play soccer in his youth. His dad also made him join Indian Guides which was similar to Boy Scouts. A famous story about Matt that I have heard over and over again is this. When Matt was about seven years old he yelled, "All I do at school is work, work, work; then I come home and have to YELL to be heard, then I have to go to dumb old Indian Guides."

I discovered that our families had many similarities. Matt and I both grew up in wonderful, loving Christian homes. We both attended a Lutheran church. We both witnessed our parents serving others in the church and community. We both shared the same viewpoint on marriage and the different roles and responsibilities of the husband and wife. The weekend was a success but it came to an end much too fast.

I was invited to spend Memorial Day weekend with his family at their cottage in Traverse City. My mother wasn't sure that was a good idea. She asked, "What if you end up not liking him? You will be stuck there for the whole weekend."

I said, "I love his sister so if things don't work out with Matt then I will hang out with Carolyn."

Carolyn and I drove up to the cottage together. Wonderful conversation made the four hour car ride fly by. Upon our arrival, we were greeted with warm hugs from Matt and his parents. Matt's mom showed me around the cottage. What a cozy, little place full of love and family memories. I loved seeing all the picture collages that Matt's dad had made. Mrs. Matzinger took great pride in showing me the dollhouse that Mr. Matzinger had made for her. I quickly found out it was off limits to play with because of how special it was to her.

I was eager to hear the story behind the dollhouse. One day out of the blue Mr. Matzinger asked Mrs. Matzinger, "What is something I can get for you? What is something you have always wanted?"

She answered, "I wanted a dollhouse when I was a young girl but due to The Depression my family could not afford one. I would love to finally be able to have my very own dollhouse." Mr. Matzinger went to the store to buy a dollhouse kit and built this dollhouse with love. Mrs. Matzinger had a fabulous time buying people and furnishings for it. Her childhood wish had come true.

After getting a full tour of the cottage, Matt and I had a blast swimming and boating. In the late evening, we would sit out on the dock and look up at the stars. How romantic! Matt took me on walks so we could have some alone time. Conversation came easy and we filled each other in on our high school years. I could tell Matt was ambitious, intelligent and unique which were qualities I admired.

We didn't realize it at the time, but we were both self-centered instead of God-centered. We talked about our own hopes and dreams instead of asking God what He had planned for our lives. Our faith was there, it was just immature. A special friendship had developed over the weekend and I left the cottage wearing Matt's class ring.

Matt was finishing his freshman year at Northwestern Michigan College in Traverse City, when our courtship began. It was the spring of 1988. A couple months later as we were sitting in the movie theater waiting for the show to start, Matt sprang some news on me. He said, "I plan to complete two years of college and then enlist in the Marine Corps."

I was not happy with this news as my plan was to never date anyone in the military. "Why would you want to do that?" I asked.

He firmly said, "It is something I have always felt called to do." My brain was working overtime trying to figure out a way to make him change his mind. My thoughts were that once he falls madly in love with me he will not want to leave me to join the Marines. However, once I got to know him better, I knew his mind was made up and I was not going to be able to change it.

Our relationship continued with a few rocky moments. He broke up with me at one point. I was absolutely crushed as I really felt that Matt was the one I was going to marry. It was a time of despair for me. I had put my hope in my future with Matt instead of putting my hope in God and trusting Him with my future. If only I had mastered the concept that hope in anything other than God would lead to disappointment.

A few weeks later Matt called asking me to get back together with him. Our relationship grew more serious over the course of the next year. Matt finished up his two years of college and moved down to Rochester, Michigan to spend the summer living closer to me. Our entire relationship had been long-distance and we needed this time together before Matt entered the Marine Corps. A family from church offered to rent out a room to him.

It was a tough summer on our relationship. Matt was working a landscaping job so he was exhausted at the end of the day and wanted to stay indoors in air conditioning. I was working indoors all day at a bank headquarters and wanted to spend the evenings outdoors being active. I ended up breaking up with him. I had thought that our differences had become more of a burden than a benefit to our relationship.

Matt had the opposite point of view. He explained how our differences complimented one another and that we were a good team. Our differences were minor compared to our mutual core values. We had a long talk and ended up getting back together. At the end of the summer he moved back up to Traverse City with our relationship intact.

In September 1989, Matt told me he had enlisted in the Marine Corps. We were driving in his pick-up truck helping his sister, Kathleen, move into a new house when he proudly announced, "I made it official today. I signed the papers at the recruiter's office."

I know I should have been proud of him and happy for him but I remember wanting to cry. I knew how hard it was to have a four hour long-distance relationship. I certainly did not want any further miles to separate us.

I kept reminding myself that one of the things I loved about Matt was his ambition and his love for adventure. I knew I couldn't keep him from following his dream and doing what he was called to do. We were too much in love at this point to even consider breaking up until after his enlistment so we promised that we would make this work. In December 1989, Matt headed to San Diego for Marine Corps boot camp with my full support.

Right away his parents and I began planning our trip to California to see Matt graduate from boot camp. Matt was able to receive mail but not too much at once or else he paid for it with push-ups. I saved every letter he sent me. I would not have lasted one day in boot camp. To everyone who has endured this tough training, I salute you.

My family was entertained as I would share some of the letters Matt wrote to me. We were all very proud of Matt and prayed that God would give him the strength needed to survive basic training. We were also feeling sorry for Matt with some of the crazy things Matt had to do. Matt would have to yell, "Permission to use the head, Sir!" In other words, he couldn't just wake up in the morning and use the bathroom. He had to yell for permission. Eating was not a pleasant experience either. He could not talk to anyone. He had to stare at his food. He learned to eat as fast as he could because he never knew how long he would have. If one of the recruits messed up in any way, then they were all done eating.

Before I knew it, I was on a plane headed to San Diego. It turned out to be a pleasant week-long vacation with my boyfriend's parents. We got along great but they were overprotective of me. We were shopping in a small antique store and I was a couple aisles away from the Matzingers. Mrs. Matzinger yelled, "Karen, where are you?"

I just laughed and said, "Right over here."

She said, 'Well don't wander off too far."

I didn't say this out loud but I was thinking, "Okay, I am a twenty-year-old, not a two-year-old. We are in a tiny shop. Where do you think I am going to go?"

On our second day in San Diego we were able to go to a church service with Matt. This was our first chance to see Matt since he left for boot camp three months earlier. I wanted to take my time and get myself beautiful for him. I thought we had plenty of time because church didn't start for about two hours. Next thing I knew, the Matzingers were asking me if I was ready. I wasn't prepared to leave so early. My hair was still wet so I quickly put it in a french braid and out the door we went. I soon learned that the Matzingers like to arrive very early, whereas I usually show up right on time.

I still remember standing outside the building and seeing Matt and about six other Marines in uniform marching up to us. Matt looked more handsome than ever. I wanted to hug him but he was not allowed to hug so we just smiled and said, "Hi." I was the only girl in church and I was surrounded by two dozen eighteen to twenty-two year old Marines. Talk about every single girl's dream. I don't remember anything about the sermon that day. We came back in the afternoon for family visitation day. We said our good-byes and then the Matzingers and I spent the week sightseeing, while Matt finished up his final five days of boot camp.

Finally, the day of boot camp graduation was upon us. Watching the Marines in their dress blues march past us was quite a sight. It was the most patriotic ceremony I had ever experienced. After graduation Matt was dismissed and we could take him off base. Matt's twenty-first birthday occurred during boot camp so we took him to a nice restaurant and Matt's parents bought him a drink.

Matt was given thirty days leave before returning for Marine Combat Training. Boot camp had matured Matt and he became even more of a gentleman. Matt shared with me how he found comfort in talking to the Chaplain and attending church services. Boot camp was just as mentally exhausting as it was physically exhausting. When the drill sergeant was tearing him down mentally, Matt remained focused on who he was in God's eyes. I was proud of Matt. I wanted to spend as much time with him as I could. I remained hopeful that it wouldn't be too long before we could see each other again.

CHAPTER 3

Surprises Bring Hope

Months went by and our relationship continued to grow stronger. We wrote letters and talked on the phone at least once a week. Matt was very interested in hearing about my days as a college student at Concordia College which is now Concordia University in Ann Arbor, Michigan. I loved the dorm life. My Elementary Education classes were going well, at least in the beginning.

One of my class requirements, during my second semester, was to spend four hours a week in a second grade classroom as the teacher's assistant. I looked forward to going each week. I realized that being a teacher's assistant was a great fit for me but being a teacher would be much more challenging. The teacher I was working with told me she felt I lacked the initiative needed to be a teacher. She loved how I followed her directions and how I worked well in small groups but she wanted to see me take charge of the classroom.

I was uncertain as to what my role was because I had just begun taking the Elementary Education classes and this wasn't

18

student teaching. This class was about getting experience in the classroom. Once again I found myself listening to one person's opinion of me instead of asking God what it was He wanted me to do. I continued on with the program as I was not ready to change majors just yet but my enthusiasm had been calmed.

Matt came home for a week at Christmas. The day after he flew in, he asked me to go ring shopping with him. "Breathe, Karen, breathe." I found the ring of my dreams. We went back to his sister Joanna's house and told the family what we had just been shopping for. There were a lot of cheering and hugs. I noticed that they did not seem all that surprised. Apparently Matt had asked their opinion on what kind of ring I would want. I was so thankful Matt decided to let me pick it out because when his sisters showed me their choices, it did not match my taste at all.

I was a bit disappointed in that I still hadn't received an official marriage proposal. I suppose we were engaged because we went ring shopping but I wanted to be asked. Matt wanted to ask me on Christmas Eve after church. He was wearing his dress blues and he knew how much I loved that uniform. He kept asking me to take a walk with him. I kept refusing because it was so cold outside. Finally, on Christmas day when we were alone he got down on one knee and asked me to marry him. I was disappointed that there was no surprise factor or no romantic story to share about the proposal. However, I was floating on cloud nine because I was engaged to my love, my handsome Marine.

The rest of our time together was fantastic. We went back and forth between my house and his parents' house. There were several friends and family members who we wanted to spend time with. Everyone wanted a wedding date but we weren't ready to set one. I wasn't sure what my future college plans entailed. Matt still had three years left of his enlistment and he wasn't sure when he would be scheduled for his six month overseas duty.

Much too soon it was time to say good-bye again. I hated those hard good-byes, crying at the airport wondering how long it would be until we saw each other again. Matt flew back to Twentynine Palms, California where he worked as a telephone/radio repair technician and I headed back to college. What exciting news I had to share with all the girls in my dorm. I kept staring at my ring thinking, *Wow! A diamond. This means forever.*

In February of 1991, Matt called me with some upsetting news. "Karen, I just received orders to join my unit in Kuwait."

With tears streaming down my face I asked, "When do you leave?"

Matt replied, "I do not have an exact date yet but probably sometime in March." Matt tried to comfort me but I was quite upset. Then he said, "Karen, this is what I have been trained to do. This is the reality of my job. Instead of worrying about me, pray for me. I love you."

I was devastated. I ran to my friend Chris's dorm room and she just held me. Her fiancé was currently over there so she knew all too well the emotions that were going through me. She was full of comfort and encouragement. Chris told me that I had to put Matt in God's hands or else I would spend every waking moment worried about his safety. She told me to stay busy and to stay focused on my job as a student. "As hard as it may be, Karen, you need to remain upbeat when you talk to Matt on the phone. He will have plenty of things on his mind. You can help him by being strong so that he won't have to worry about you.

Also, limit the amount of time you spend watching the news about the war. Do not isolate yourself. You need to be able to talk to your friends about your feelings. Send care packages and be active in supporting the troops. My biggest advice, Karen, is to pray."

She helped me call my mom. I couldn't even get the words out so she reached for the phone and told my mom the news. For the remainder of the week, I was not functioning well. I asked one of my professors for an extension on a speech that was coming due. She was very understanding and gave me the extra time to come to grips with all this. If only I had been able to listen to Chris and hand all my worries over to God. As I look back I can say, "I worried for nothing."

I will never forget February 27, 1991. I was on the other side of campus watching television with a group of students. We had just heard the announcement that the Persian Gulf War was over. We were jumping up and down with excitement. My roommate came running up to me with the message that Matt had called. She said he would be calling back at ten o'clock sharp. I ran back to the room awaiting his phone call. Right around ten o'clock at night, there was a knock on our door. I opened the door and screamed. All the girls in my dorm came running to see what was wrong.

Standing there in his dress blues was Matt. We just stood there hugging and kissing with all the girls watching us. Everyone was crying including me. I stared at him and kept saying, "I can't believe you are here."

He said, "Surprise, I am home for one month." A smile was glued to my face as I stared at Matt. I may not have had a surprise marriage proposal but I sure received my romantic surprise.

Fortunately, Matt's twin sisters, Joanna and Carolyn, lived just fifteen minutes away from my college campus so Matt stayed with them. They let Matt borrow their car whenever they weren't using it. It was exciting to show Matt around campus and introduce him to all my friends. I had a hard time concentrating on school work. As always, our time together flew by and before we knew it we were kissing good-bye.

I finished the school year at Concordia College and decided not to return in the fall. I was lacking the confidence and the determination needed to continue pursuing my dream of becoming a teacher. Feeling lost in what direction my future would take, I tried figuring it out myself instead of asking God. My number one goal was to be married to Matt so I could see him every day.

In June I helped Matt pull off another one of his surprises. He wanted to be in Traverse City to see his mom graduate with an Associate Degree in Liberal Arts. I was the only one who knew he was coming. When we knocked on the Matzinger's front door, Mrs. Matzinger almost fell backwards when she saw Matt. The look on her face was priceless.

Having put all five of her children through college, she decided it was her turn. Mrs. Matzinger was in her sixties and it was a dream of hers to earn a college degree. She was beaming as she walked across the stage to receive her diploma. Her children and grandchildren were clapping and cheering with pride and enthusiasm. We had a graduation party for her and then went back to the cottage to swim. A few days later Matt and I said another tearful good-bye at the airport.

I was once again living at home and was looking for a part-time job. I enrolled at a community college to finish my Associate Degree in Liberal Arts. I took evening classes so that I could spend my days babysitting for a four month old girl named Jenny. She brought so much joy into my life. It was a job I loved so much, that I would have gladly worked without pay if I could have afforded to do so.

During the next eleven months Matt and I saw each other a few times but still did not have a wedding date set. We didn't want to wait until his enlistment was done so we discussed getting married the next time he came home on leave. Matt and I were longing for the security that marriage brings to a relationship. We were feeling the strain of the long-distance. Our love was strong, but we were burned out from being apart for months at a time.

We were young, immature and in love and so we came up with a crazy plan.

Matt was scheduled to come home in June of 1992 for his parent's 40th wedding anniversary celebration. We had decided several weeks before that we were just going to get married when he came home. Loving surprises, Matt suggested that we not tell anyone of our plans. I hesitantly said, "Okay." How does a girl keep her upcoming wedding a secret? Somehow I managed not to say anything.

My parents informed me that they were going down to Georgia to attend their godchild's high school graduation. "Yikes! My parents will be out of town when I get married. What do I do now?" I decided to stick with Matt on the secrecy issue.

Matt arrived in Michigan and two days later on June 5, 1992, we walked into the assistant pastor's office and handed him a piece of paper. My dad was the senior pastor at our church. The assistant pastor said, "This looks like a marriage license." The pastor was expecting us to come in for pre-marriage counseling because that is what I said when I made the appointment with him the week before.

Matt said, "We want to get married today."

Pastor's response, "What? Um, Karen, your parents are out of town. You want me to marry you now?"

"Yes", we said smiling.

"I'm not sure this is a good idea," he said frantically. He began pacing. Finally the pastor said, "I know you are both of legal age and do not need your parents' permission to do this, but for the sake of keeping peace in your families, will you please call and tell them what you are about to do?" We both agreed that was a wise idea. Matt was twenty-three at the time and I was a month shy of twenty-three. I went first.

"Hi Mom. I have some news. Matt and I are at church about to get married."

"WHAT? Can't you at least wait until we get home?" She tearfully asked.

I responded, "No mom, we can't. You and dad will not be home until Monday and Matt leaves on Tuesday. It has to be today."

Realizing our minds were made up, she pleaded, "Can you at least make sure Peter and Sarah (my younger brother and sister) are with you?"

"Yes Mom. We can do that," I said.

"Okay, I don't think I can talk anymore," my mom said as she hung up the phone.

Maybe this wasn't such a good idea, I momentarily think. This wasn't the way I had envisioned my wedding day at all. My dream wedding included my dad walking me down the aisle and then performing the wedding ceremony. My mom would be smiling at everyone. I would be wearing a beautiful white wedding gown. My sisters would be bridesmaids and my brother Peter would be a groomsman. Two hundred friends and family members would be gathered around. This day was far from that dream.

I gave the phone to Matt and he dialed his parent's number. "Hi, Mom. Are you sitting down? Go get Dad and sit down. Trust me. You will want to be sitting down for this news."

Matt's mom replied, "Okay we are both on the phone. What is it?"

"Karen and I are getting married," Matt announced enthusiastically.

"When?" asked Matt's mom.

"As soon as I get off the phone with you."

Matt's mom squealed with delight. "Oh, Oh, Oh! We are so happy for you both. Let us talk to Karen."

I nervously said, "Hi."

Mr. and Mrs. Matzinger said in unison, "Oh, Karen. We love you. We are so happy that you and Matt are getting married."

The pastor was still pretty nervous at this point. I'm sure he enjoyed the break as we left to go find Peter and Sarah. Peter was at home so that was easy. Sarah had gone shopping at a store right by the church. We searched the store but couldn't find her. I walked into the fitting room. "Sarah, are you in here?"

"Yes, I'm right here. Who is this?"

"It's your sister," I said.

"I don't have a sister," she replied.

"Oh, sorry. Wrong Sarah." And I ran out of there. We tried the house again and this time she was home. "Peter and Sarah, we need you to come to church with us. We are getting married right now."

"What? Are you two crazy?" Peter and Sarah asked.

"Yes we are. Come on." Matt and I said eagerly.

There we were standing in the chapel with pastor, Peter and Sarah. In all the craziness we didn't think to include my older sister, Jennifer. We didn't even take any pictures that day. I wore a short sleeve navy sweater top and white skirt. Matt had on white pants and a casual blue silk shirt. Peter and Sarah had on shorts and a T-shirt. Not exactly your dream wedding attire. Not exactly your dream wedding. In the small chapel at St. John Lutheran Church in Rochester, Michigan, Matt and I each said, "I do."

As we signed the marriage license, the church secretary gave us all the cash she had in her wallet and told us to go out to a nice dinner. We went back to my house, dropped off Peter and Sarah, and packed our suitcases. My grandmother was living with us at the time. We told her our big news. She said she could tell something fishy was going on. She hugged us and told us that she and grandpa had gotten married on June 5th as well. Matt put the suitcases in the car and we were off to spend our wedding night at a luxurious hotel.

The next day we had to report to Matt's sister Joanna's house to help set up for the anniversary party. We told his sisters our news. They were quite surprised but happy for us. Although we were newlyweds we still had to help clean the house for the party. We made a fun day out of it.

We went to Sunday morning service the next day. The pastor prayed for blessing on Pastor and Peggy Burow who were out of town for the weekend. And then he prayed for blessing on the marriage of Matthew Matzinger and Karen Burow that had just taken place. Matt and I looked at each other as we heard the stunned reaction from the entire congregation.

My friends came up to hug us. Some of them were sad that they weren't included. Some were happy for us and understood why we did what we did. A few friends thought we were crazy. Many people waited until my parents were back in town to get the scoop from them. Some wanted to know if my mom and dad were furious with us. My parents told people that they were not angry with the news and that the quick wedding was actually their idea. However, my mom and dad were surprised with the timing of the wedding and wished they could have been there.

The anniversary party for Matt's parents was next on our agenda. I was introduced as Matt's wife! The guests looked confused. It was fun to share our news of the surprise wedding. Immediately following the anniversary party Matt and I headed to the cottage to have a two day honeymoon. It was fantastic being at the cottage for the first time as husband and wife.

Matt flew back to California on Tuesday evening, and I remained in Michigan. Being married made our good-bye easier.

I had the hope of a wonderful future with Matt. We decided that I would not move out to California right away. Matt would soon be heading to Okinawa for his six months of overseas duty. We both agreed that I would be happier living with my parents while he was gone instead of being in California by myself. We were finally married, but still living apart. Our plan of being together did not work out so well but I was able to make two trips to see Matt that I couldn't have made had we not been married.

Two months after our wedding, I flew to California for a ten day visit with Matt. We went to Universal Studios, Palm Springs, and Joshua Tree National Park. Matt gave me a lesson on his motor bike/motorcycle. Matt was a great teacher but I just wasn't feeling very comfortable driving it. I enjoyed the comfort of riding on the back holding tight to Matt.

I made another quick trip to see Matt in November. We went to the Marine Corps Ball which is a ceremony to celebrate the birthday of the Marine Corps. Earlier in the day I had gone to the hair salon for an 'up do'. I wore a floor length black formal gown and Matt wore his dress blues. We arrived at the end of the cocktail hour. Then the Marines all stood at attention for the Presentation of the Colors and for the National Anthem. Next, the Marine Corps Hymn was played while a few Marines brought out the large birthday cake. We enjoyed a delicious steak dinner. After dinner, Matt and I danced the night away. It was a night to remember. The entire weekend was fabulous and we were looking forward to seeing each other again in five weeks.

Matt came home as scheduled for Christmas and New Year's. It was our first Christmas as husband and wife. Matt took me in his arms and we danced to the music of our hearts. He told me how much he loved me and how right it felt being married. He told me how eager he was to get the chance to take care of me once we were finally living together. Matt voiced his appreciation for how supportive I was of him and how comforting it was knowing that he had me to come home to. "This is it, Karen. We only have six more months of being apart and then no more long tearful good-byes."

In February of 1993, Matt left for Okinawa for his six month overseas tour of duty. Matt was looking forward to seeing a different part of the world. He took advantage of the beautiful beaches and learned how to scuba dive. Scuba diving became a new passion for him. Although I was missing him, I was also full of hope thinking that this would be the final chapter of our long-distance relationship.

Back on the home front I continued to babysit for Jenny. I was also making plans for our renewal of vows ceremony so that I could still have my dream wedding. My parents were very supportive of that idea and they helped me plan a regular wedding reception. I went shopping for a wedding gown but ended up borrowing one. We hired a florist and a disc jockey. A family friend made the wedding cake as a gift and my uncle agreed to be our official photographer. It was an exciting time planning it all. We set the date for August 27, 1993 because Matt would be home from Japan by then.

In late spring I had an amazing opportunity to take a trip to Japan with other military wives. We were allowed to visit our husbands for eleven days. I flew to Los Angeles where I met the other wives. Everyone was so nice and we all had so much in common. After the eleven hour plane ride, we arrived in Tokyo. We had to carry our luggage upstairs, downstairs and then climb up and down more stairs. The stairs seemed endless but we finally managed to squeeze on to the crowded subway. We were quite a sight. Can you picture twenty-five American ladies dragging their luggage through the Tokyo subway system during morning rush hour? We were in everyone's way. With no time to spare, we made it on the plane. Now we could relax for the two and a half hour plane ride to Okinawa.

It was time for our joyful reunion. Other than the time when Matt had to work, we were inseparable. The base was beautiful with the palm trees and beaches. I didn't care for the Japanese food, so we ate most of our meals on the American base. Matt and I celebrated our one year anniversary in Japan. We did a lot of sightseeing but the highlight of the trip was just being with Matt.

It was an easy good-bye this time knowing that this was our last good-bye. I was preparing to move to California and would arrive before Matt's unit returned. In less than two months we would be together and our long-distance misery would FINALLY come to an end. No more letter writing or late night phone calls. Having been married for more than one year, we were finally going to get to live together. The hope of a bright and wonderful future lay before us.

CHAPTER 4

A MARRIAGE FULL OF HOPE

When Matt's unit arrived at the base, I was there with open
arms to welcome him home. What a joyous reunion we had! We
were newlyweds and very much in love. We lived in a tiny two
bedroom apartment but it was our home. For the first few weeks
all we had were our clothes and a bed. Our bridal shower gifts and
furniture had not arrived from Michigan yet. After one week of
eating on the floor, I splurged and bought two cheap lawn chairs
and T.V. trays.

We both enjoyed being outdoors, despite the heat. I loved
rollerblading and so Matt was willing to try it. We bought a pair
of rollerblades and elbow pads for him and I taught him the basic
skills. He wiped out pretty good on the day that he forgot to put
on the elbow pads. I went to help him up and grabbed the part
of his arm that was scraped. I joined him on the ground and we
both started laughing.

Matt loved rock climbing at Joshua Tree National Park which
was only twenty minutes away from our apartment. I was willing
to try it but nothing too dangerous. We had a lot of fun and my

confidence and courage had improved within a few months. We also enjoyed the times when friends would join us on the rocks. Our friends had two young boys with them so obviously our rock climbing wasn't very intense.

We both loved listening to country music and we would drive an hour to go country line dancing. Matt was much better at dancing than I was. He was very patient and had to teach me several of the dance steps. I would finally catch on to the dance moves just as the song was ending.

Palm Springs was an hour drive and so we took many day trips there. We loved seeing the green grass and green trees. Living in Twentynine Palms, we were surrounded by sand and desert. In August and September the daily average temperature was still in the 90s and 100s. By evening, it cooled down to the high 80s and we would often take walks. This was my favorite time of day, walking hand in hand with Matt. It was fantastic to finally be together.

Matt and I flew back to Michigan at the end of August for our renewal of vows ceremony. The morning of the ceremony Matt and I were at the chiropractor's office. I had severe back pain from all the stress of wanting the day to be perfect. Matt was wearing his dress blues and I was wearing my veil as I had just come from the hair salon. The patients in the waiting room congratulated us and let us go ahead of them.

Upon arriving at the church I was able to relax. My five bridesmaids looked beautiful in their wine colored floor length dresses. Matt and I stood in the back of the church waiting to walk in together. At the appropriate time Matt yelled, "Congregation, a-ten-hut!" We then walked down the aisle to "Battle Hymn of the Republic".

It was a beautiful ceremony with my dad officiating and two hundred guests celebrating with us. My dream wedding had come true after all. When the ceremony ended and pictures were taken, we enjoyed a delicious buffet dinner. After dinner, Matt and I danced to all our favorite songs including a few country line dances. As we were leaving, Matt picked me up in his arms and I told him, "I love you, honey, with all my heart. I just had the time of my life but I know the best is yet to come."

The following day we gathered at my parents' house to open up all our wedding gifts. We spent a few days visiting with family and friends. Then it was time to head back to California. After all the years of flying alone, we treasured this time of traveling together.

We were growing as a couple and discovering new things about each other. As happy as we were, we did have our moments of disagreements. Matt teased me that I had to have the apartment in perfect order before company came over. He left his shoes by the door and I wanted to move them to our bedroom. He told me that his shoes were staying put and that our friends wouldn't notice or even care about his shoes. We both started laughing about how uptight I was.

Some of our arguments were regarding more serious matters. Matt and I discovered that it would have been helpful to have had pre-marriage counseling. Money was a source of conflict. We quickly found out that I was the saver and Matt was the spender. A new budget was formed and we both agreed to stick to it.

Matt's enlistment ended in December of 1993. We briefly considered staying in Southern California but we prayed about it and decided to move to Michigan to be closer to family. Friends helped us clean out our apartment and pack up the moving truck. Matt and I took turns driving across the country. Instead of sightseeing, our goal was to make this a quick trip. We surprised our family by arriving in Michigan one full day ahead of schedule.

My parents graciously let us live with them while Matt and I searched for jobs. It was a full house with my Mom, Dad, Peter, Sarah, Grandma, Matt, and I. After being on our own, it was a struggle to adjust to living under my parents' roof again. We were incredibly thankful for their hospitality but we were hopeful that this would be very short-term.

A friend helped me get a job in a large company working in accounts receivable. Accounting had been one of my favorite subjects and I enjoyed working with debits and credits. A few months later Matt found a decent job as an assistant plant manager for a small manufacturing company. As soon as he received his first paycheck we moved into an apartment. It felt great to be living on our own again.

Our next order of business was to find a new church. Matt and I wanted a smaller church than the one where my dad was pastor. Also we wanted to be known as Matt and Karen not as the pastor's daughter and her husband. We found a great church with a contemporary service. Matt and I felt God leading us to help with the youth ministry. We enjoyed organizing fun events like volleyball, softball, horseback riding, and service projects.

Matt missed the military and decided to join the Army National Guard and train with the military police. I didn't mind because he would only be gone one weekend a month and two weeks in the summer. He also went back to school at night to work towards his bachelor's degree in Criminal Justice Administration. Matt had always had an interest in criminal justice and now he was pursuing his passion.

Another change for us was the decision to buy a condominium. We moved into our condo and bought a puppy all in the same week. We instantly fell in love with Simba, our eight week old yellow Labrador retriever, the moment we saw him. Simba was the first dog I ever had. Matt had a few dogs throughout his childhood so he was completely at ease with how to handle a puppy. I wanted to quit my job and stay home with "my baby" but Matt didn't go for that. Matt assured me that Simba would be fine in his crate all day and that Matt would come home on his lunch hour to check on him.

Another change came a few months later. In early December of 1995, Matt received a phone call saying that his National Guard unit had orders to go to Germany for up to nine months. He left one week before Christmas. I couldn't stop crying. I thought we were done with the long-distance hassle. I didn't have any energy left to deal with it again. My boss gave me a week off work and I flew down to Texas to spend Christmas with my Dad, Mom, Peter and Sarah. My parents had recently moved to San Antonio.

I found comfort in the fact that Matt was stationed in Germany and not Bosnia. The United States and Allied Nations deployed peacekeeping forces to Bosnia in support of Operation Joint Endeavor. Several of the troops who were stationed in Germany were sent to Bosnia and therefore, Matt's unit needed to offer back-up support in Germany. Matt was assigned to an American base doing routine military police work so I was not worried about his safety. I just missed him terribly.

Matt asked me to come over and visit him, so in March I flew to Germany. We had one week together and toured Germany, Austria, and Switzerland. We took a chairlift to the top of the Swiss Alps and I danced around singing songs from *The Sound of Music*. Matt was enjoying the beautiful view but I did see him glance my way and smile. The way he smiled at me made me feel like we were still newlyweds. Next thing I knew, we were back at the airport with another tearful good-bye.

While Matt was in Germany I continued to be the youth leader at our church. I also took a few evening classes towards my bachelor's degree. In addition, I made the decision to leave my office job and spend my days babysitting. I had two potential job offers and wasn't sure which one to take. I remember praying, "Lord, please hit me over the head with which job would be the right fit. Please make it clear to me as to where you want me to be. Give the families interviewing me the wisdom to know what to do also."

I love how God answered this prayer. I was very excited about the first family even though they needed me to be very flexible with my hours. Being a very scheduled person, this job wasn't the best fit for me but I couldn't see that at the time. As I was walking out the door to meet the other family, the phone rang. God told me to answer the phone even if that meant being late to the interview. The first family was calling to tell me that they were very impressed with me but that they decided to give their current nanny another chance.

Arriving on time to my next interview, I had the hope that this was the job God wanted me to have. I was extremely impressed with this Christian family and was thrilled when they offered me the job. In no time at all I became very attached to JD, a two and a half year old, and his nine month old sister Megan. JD and Megan were very sweet and well behaved children. They were on a great schedule and I learned a lot about parenting from both their mom and dad. I felt like part of their family.

A few weeks later, Matt came home. It wasn't as easy of a transition as we were anticipating. It took us about three months to get acclimated to living together again. We felt this was normal for most military couples who had been separated but we still decided to go to marriage counseling. Our counselor happened to be a former military chaplain. He was very easy to talk to and Matt and I looked forward to our sessions.

One of the things our counselor recommended was that we go on dates and just have fun together. He also told us to quit giving each other the silent treatment when we felt angry at each other. We needed to talk out our differences instead of avoiding them. Another problem was the fact that neither Matt nor I had many close friendships. It was unfair to rely on each other as our only source of companionship. We needed friends. A spouse cannot fill your every need. No one can fill your every need but God.

We had spent months and years praying for friends. We were getting discouraged and began questioning God as to why He wasn't placing friends in our life. Matt was working at a small company and he didn't have much in common with his few co-workers. I was babysitting so I didn't have any co-workers. Most of the families at church had children and we wanted to find another couple like us who didn't have children yet. I can now see how our prayers were about asking God to bless our plans and criteria for friends instead of being open to what God had in mind. With the exception of our wonderful neighbor who would walk her dog with us every day, the few friends we did have lived out of town.

Another issue that was brought up was Matt's state of unhappiness. Many times I would tell Matt to enjoy the moment instead of always looking ahead. Our counselor didn't spend much time on this issue. In hindsight I believe Matt was suffering from depression. Unfortunately, Matt's depression would continue to go untreated for several more years until one day the help would come but it would be too little too late.

Our finances were probably the number one source of conflict in our marriage. Matt would use credit cards irresponsibly, see the error of his ways, cut up the cards, vow to change, and then start all over again. I had asked him several times to go to financial seminars on budgeting but he wouldn't go. I came close to calling his parents a few times to ask them to talk to him but the fear of admitting we had problems prevented me from making the phone call.

Through a lot of tears and a lot of prayers, I remained hopeful that Matt would change. Matt was sincere in his efforts, I had no doubt about that. Our counselor encouraged Matt to change his spending habits and it worked for a while. Matt needed that accountability which made me regret not telling anyone other than our counselor. Once we were done with counseling, Matt lost the accountability and resumed his old spending habits.

Matt and I were very encouraged regarding other areas within our marriage. Our counselor had us each write down five goals that we had for the next three years. Without looking at what each other wrote, we had to guess the answers. Matt and I both guessed correctly and our counselor was impressed with how well we knew each other's goals and dreams. It was a mutual decision to end counseling after about six sessions.

Within the next year Matt's schedule eased up. His enlistment with the National Guard was done and I was relieved. Matt had earned his degree in Criminal Justice Administration. Matt supported my decision to go back to school. I was working toward my bachelor's degree in Family Life Education. The classes were in the evening which worked out great with my babysitting schedule.

We decided to get a second dog so that Simba would have a playmate. In our opinion, Simba was the world's greatest dog and we were hoping to get another dog just like him. We chose a female yellow Labrador retriever and named her Jasmine. She was absolutely adorable but was spunkier than Simba had ever been. Having two dogs chasing each other around our condo probably wasn't the wisest idea we had. We had also forgotten what it was like having a puppy that woke us up at night to go outside. It was winter which made it worse. Matt let me stay in our warm, cozy bed and he would volunteer to take Jasmine out.

Another change that occurred was Matt's decision to leave the manufacturing business. He found a great job at a large telecommunications company. Even though he took a slight pay cut, he was hopeful that he would be able to move up in the company. Matt was well trained in telecommunications from his days in the Marine Corps and he really enjoyed this new position.

Matt was always willing to learn and be active in the church. He made a two year commitment to be involved in Stephen Ministry. A Stephen Minister provides one-on-one Christian care to individuals who are going through a difficult time. Upon completing his fifty hours of training, he was assigned a care receiver. Matt would meet with this individual on a weekly basis. Matt provided a caring and confidential listening ear and spiritual encouragement. Confidentiality was an important factor and Matt was not allowed to share the name of the individual with me or the circumstances involved. I respected Matt for his ability to honor this commitment.

Matt and I had a full schedule but we both decided it was time to start a family. I had less than a year left of school so we thought that even if I got pregnant right away, the timing would be perfect. Within the month I took a pregnancy test and it was positive. I sat in the hallway near the bathroom and cried for about thirty minutes. I thanked God for the miracle growing inside me. Then I touched my stomach and said, "Hi baby. I am your mom and I already love you so much."

When the joyful tears finally stopped I called Matt and asked him to come home for lunch. It was a quick conversation because I could hardly contain my joy but I wanted to be able to surprise him and tell him in person. As soon as Matt opened the front door I ran into his arms and joyfully announced, 'We're going to have a baby!"

Matt smiled from ear to ear and said, "Oh Karen, I am so happy. I can't believe this happened so fast. We are going to be parents. May God grant us wisdom." We both thanked God and could hardly eat because of the excitement. Matt wanted to stay home with me to celebrate but he had to get back to work. After work he took me to our favorite restaurant.

I loved being pregnant and couldn't wait to buy maternity clothes. Matt took extra good care of me. He would rub my swollen feet and massage my back almost every night. I did not want to know the sex of the baby but Matt did. Matt came with me to the ultrasound and the technician wrote the sex of our baby on a piece of paper and handed it to Matt. He was able to keep it a surprise from me for the duration of the pregnancy.

During the last half of my pregnancy I was babysitting three days a week, finishing classes, and doing an internship two days a week. I had the privilege of working with a Family Life Minister at a local Lutheran church. He had been my high school youth director and was willing to allow me the opportunity to learn from him as well as work with him. My main assignment was to research ideas for an upcoming marriage retreat and then I worked with him in planning the entire retreat. It was a great experience for me and I was wondering how God was going to use me in the future.

I finished my internship in January and completed my course work in March of 1999. I did it! Despite the fact I was once told not to bother applying to college, here I was graduating with honors. I had earned my Bachelor's Degree in Family Life Education. Now I had one month to relax before our baby was born.

During a weekly doctor appointment in early April, my doctor informed me that my baby was breech. I cried all the way home from the appointment because I did not want to have a C-section. This was not the way I had planned it! I was angry with God. Matt tried to comfort me. My mom tried to comfort me. Once again, God was about to show me that His way was best.

CHAPTER 5

CLINGING TO HOPE

On April 15, 1999 Matt drove me to the hospital for the scheduled C-section. The doctor cut me open and told me that he could see the baby's head. I was so excited and nervous that I asked if the baby was a boy or girl. Everyone in the operating room laughed and said, "We can't tell from the head." At 8:46 P.M. our precious Eric Paul was born. He was the most beautiful baby I had ever seen. Tears of joy were streaming down my face. I couldn't wait to hold Eric. Matt was beaming as he cut the umbilical cord. My arms were still strapped down to the table but Matt brought Eric over to me so I could look at him and kiss his precious face.

Matt left the hospital around midnight thinking everything was fine. I had a problem with fluid in my lungs so I was moved to intensive care. Doctors and nurses were doing several tests on me. Around two o'clock in the morning I had had enough. I lost my patience and yelled, "Everyone stop touching me. Someone go bring me my baby. I haven't had the chance to hold him yet and I want him!"

The doctors looked concerned but no one told me anything. Finally, a nurse came in and told me to call Matt and have him come to the hospital right away. I was thinking that they wanted him there for me. I said, "No, I am fine. Let Matt sleep."

The nurse was persistent and called Matt. No one answered. Then I remembered I had turned off the ringer. The nurse then proceeded to call Matt's sister, Kathleen. Kathleen worked at the hospital and she lived about fifteen minutes away from our condo. Kathleen and her husband Mark drove over to the condo and pounded on the door. Matt woke up, got dressed and dashed to the hospital.

Nothing could have prepared me for the news that was about to come. Matt walked into my room with a doctor who I had never seen before. I could tell Matt had been crying. The doctor showed me a diagram of a heart and explained that Eric has a heart defect called coarctation of the aorta. They needed to transport him to Children's Hospital immediately. Matt and I just held each other and cried.

Before I even had a chance to let the news sink in, they wheeled Eric into my room. He had tubes everywhere. This can't really be happening to us. The nurse gently placed Eric in my arms. This was my first time holding him and I was wondering if it would be my last. I forced a smile for the camera because I wanted a happy picture of this moment in case it was the only picture I would have of the three of us. I kissed Eric and Matt good-bye and then I cried and cried.

Matt followed the ambulance down to Children's Hospital. Matt was given a lot of information and had to make a lot of decisions all on his own. Poor Matt. I wish I could have been there with him. Because of my own health issues following the C-section, I remained in intensive care. What a blessing that turned out to be because it would have been much too emotional to be on the maternity floor without Eric. There I lay alone in my hospital bed with my arms feeling so empty. I was tempted to ask a nurse for a baby doll to hold but decided against it.

I stared at the clock and waited until 7:00 A.M. to call my parents. I treasured sleep and couldn't stand the thought of waking anybody up. It was 6:00 A.M. in Texas so I thought that would be an okay time to call. I could hardly talk. Somehow I managed to speak the words. "Eric has to have open heart surgery." My mom started crying with me. I didn't ask her to come but the next day she was there.

Nurses are angels in more ways than one. God brought a Christian nurse to me with these words of wisdom. "Karen, thank God for the baby He gave you."

"Thank Him! Why? My baby isn't healthy," I angrily replied.

"You have no idea what God is going to do with that precious little life. He will be a blessing to you no matter what lies ahead. Do you believe in God?"

"Yes," I said.

"Then you thank God right now."

My prayer went something like this: *Thank you God! Thank you for Eric. Thank you for blessing me with the gift of a son. Thank you for your wisdom in knowing that a C-section would be easier on Eric's heart than a natural birth. Oh Great Physician, Eric is in your hands. He is in your capable, loving, almighty, healing hands. I have no control over this. You have complete control over this. I have to rest in your peace. Help me to find that peace. I ask that you would heal Eric. Heal him Lord. This is my baby. Please don't take him home yet.......... And God, thank You for the amazing way You love me. Now that I am a parent, I have a better understanding of just how much You sacrificed for me. You allowed Your one and only Son to come into a sinful world where He would be crucified.*

And You did it because of Your great love for me and for everyone. I don't want to have to give up my son - even to You – a perfect and loving God. Yet, You so freely gave up Your Son for me and for a hurting and sinful world. Thank You for making John 3:16 come to life for me. Amen.

This was the biggest lesson in trust and hope that I have had thus far. Meanwhile, Matt was exhausted. He would spend his days at Children's Hospital holding Eric and then come see me in the evenings before heading home to bed. He would bring pictures of Eric for me to have. One of the pictures showed Eric crying but Matt quickly assured me that the only reason Eric was crying at that moment was because Matt had unwrapped him for the picture. Matt was strong for me. Speaking with confidence, he would relay all the latest news regarding Eric. I was glad it was him and not me having to retell everything the doctors were saying because I just couldn't digest it all.

On April 19, 1999, our four-day-old son had open heart surgery. A neighbor friend, Mark, was with Matt as well as Matt's sister Carolyn, and my dear friend Patty. Patty was the mother of JD and Megan, the two children that I was babysitting for. Matt was quite stressed as Eric's surgery went on and on and on.

I waited anxiously for Carolyn to call me throughout the day with updates as I was still in the hospital forty-five minutes away. My mom sat with me all day and she was very comforting. She reminded me that there were more people praying for Eric than we would ever know. "Karen, Eric is in God's hands. God knows everything going on in that operating room right now. He is guiding the surgeon's hands. God already knows the outcome. God already knows all the plans He has for Eric. God knows. May peace and hope abound right now because God already knows."

The nurse approached Matt after the surgery to say that the doctor wanted to speak with him. Carolyn held Matt's hand as they walked to the private meeting room. When the surgeon saw the religious book Matt was clutching in his other hand, he asked if Matt was a Christian. He then proceeded to ask Matt if would like a word of prayer. Matt's friend Mark was with them and they all bowed their heads and the surgeon said such a lovely prayer of hope and healing for both Eric and me. Carolyn later told me that it was quite a spiritual moment.

What a relief to hear that the surgery was over and that it went very well. Our prayers were answered! The doctors sounded very optimistic that Eric would have a full recovery. We were told that there was still a minor obstruction in the mitral valve but it wasn't significant enough to repair at that time. Eric would need to have routine heart check-ups throughout his childhood.

My doctor released me that evening. I wasn't prepared for the difficulty of leaving the hospital without a baby in my arms. But, leaving the hospital meant I could go see Eric. My mom, Matt, and I went to Children's Hospital first thing in the morning. I kept telling Matt to drive faster because I couldn't contain my excitement about getting to see Eric. The wonderful nurses let me hold Eric right away. He was hooked up to many machines but he looked great. I knew he was going to be okay. Thank you God! Oh thank you God! We all took turns holding Eric but both Matt and my mom let me have the longest turn. I had a hard time letting Eric leave my arms.

Two weeks later Matt and I were given permission to take Eric home. Before leaving the hospital we had to prove we could handle taking his feeding tube in and out and also give him the appropriate medicine at the appropriate time. Matt and I prayed that God would give us the ability to be able to do all that was asked of us by the nurses. I do not handle medical issues well at all as I am very squeamish. God literally took my hands and gave me the strength and courage to handle the feeding tube. The doctors warned us of the serious consequences of not having the feeding tube in correctly. We had to use a stethoscope and listen to make sure the tube wasn't in Eric's lungs.

As soon as we arrived home, we took Eric for a walk. In a matter of weeks the feeding tube was out. Eric was growing and gaining weight and life was settling back down. We were enjoying Eric and marveling at all that God had done. Matt was a great dad. He felt comfortable changing diapers, feeding Eric, rocking Eric to sleep, and spending time alone with him while I ran errands. I was a bit overprotective as the following will prove my point.

When Eric was about eight weeks old, Matt's sister Joanna offered to watch him for a few hours. It was a beautiful sunny day so we brought Eric's stroller over to Joanna's house. Our stroller had a full canopy on it so I thoroughly explained and demonstrated how to use the canopy so that the sun would never be in Eric's eyes. Apparently, I thought a person needed to be a rocket scientist to grasp the concept of pushing a stroller with a newborn baby in it. "Now remember, when you turn the corner the sun will be in a different direction. Check Eric to make sure he is okay."

Joanna was extremely patient with me and kept saying, "Yes, Karen. I understand, Karen." Upon being completely embarrassed, Matt grabbed my hand and whisked me away on our date.

At Eric's three month heart check-up we learned that his heart was in need of repair again. On August 20th, we took Eric back to Children's Hospital for a heart catheterization. Matt's parents came with us to offer us support. The valve in Eric's aorta, which was widened during his surgery, was not growing with the rest of his heart. The doctors needed to go back in and expand it. After everything we had been through with Eric's heart surgery, we felt this was a minor procedure. This time Eric would only have to spend one night in the hospital. We were full of hope that Eric was going to be fine. Praise God that this procedure was successful.

What a blessing that I had a job where I could take Eric with me. I loved watching JD and Megan and was thrilled that I could continue on with them. JD, who was now five and Megan, who was three, treated Eric like their baby brother. Their mom turned the guest bedroom into Eric's room. From the very beginning they had treated me like family. It didn't even feel like a job to me. I loved JD and Megan like they were my own children.

A lady from church had asked me to join MOPS. MOPS stands for Mothers of Preschoolers. It is a Christian organization which is designed to meet the needs of mothers and to share the love of Christ with both the mother and her young children. At that time the group met in the morning during Eric's naptime so I did not attend. Matt and I were both into routines and kept Eric on a very tight schedule. It worked for us and we believed he was a happy child because he ate and slept at the same time every day and we believed God put something special in Eric's heart during his surgery.

The following year I was approached again about joining MOPS and being on the steering team. The lady told me to pray about it before I gave her an answer. Matt and I prayed about it and we both knew that God was leading me to accept the position of Discussion Group Leader. I would be able to apply the knowledge I gained in my Family Life Education program. Furthermore, I was trained in facilitating discussion groups.

I love how God worked out all the details. It was an added bonus that MOPS was moved to evenings at our church which worked out much better for Eric's schedule. My heart was in obedience to God and I was willing to serve Him and the other moms in this capacity. I thought I would be blessing others but God used MOPS to richly bless Matt and me instead. Through MOPS he answered our many, many years of praying for friends. I was blessed to volunteer with an amazing group of women on the steering team and they quickly became my dear friends. Matt got to know the husbands and became friends with some of them and we were both completely amazed at God's faithfulness.

Matt was doing well with his career in telecommunications. He was also taking classes toward a master's degree in computers. His new area of interest was computers and he was determined to learn more about them. Eric was now a toddler and our condo was starting to feel too small. We would love to have a yard for Eric to play in and for the dogs to run around in. We decided to put all our money into building a home. It was also time to purchase a new minivan.

I had reached a point where I had put my love for Matt and Eric ahead of my love for God. I remember this specific, honest conversation with God and exactly where I was standing in our condo. It is humbling and sad that I once had this attitude, but I did and I know God wants me to share it. "*God, I know I'm supposed to love You above all else. I don't know how to love You above my husband and son. I love them so much God. They are here with me where I can physically see them and touch them. I just don't see how it is possible to love You more.*" I did not hear any kind of a response from God at that moment.

God allowed us to temporarily continue on with **our** plan for our life. Now that we were in a four bedroom home, we decided it was time for another baby. I became pregnant immediately and we were thrilled. We prayed for a healthy pregnancy and a healthy baby. Matt and I both agreed to wait until the birth to find out if we were having a boy or a girl.

Matt was doing better in regards to his spending habits. He approached me with the idea of getting a motorcycle. Matt had been researching interstate motorcycles and found one that he really wanted. We came up with an agreement. When all our credit debt was paid in full and Matt had saved up half of the cost of the motorcycle, he could buy it. I assumed that it would take years to save up that kind of money and that Matt would learn a valuable lesson in the process.

Within a few months of this discussion we received a large income tax refund and we were able to pay off all our credit debt. One month later, Matt received a large bonus check at work that covered half the cost of the motorcycle. He was thrilled and was ready to buy the motorcycle. I was upset because the money was handed to him and he didn't have to spend time saving for it.

I was in a great women's Bible study at the time and so I asked the ladies in my group what I should do. They felt that Matt should be able to get the bike. I did not agree with them but I went along with the majority. Matt was so eager to buy it that he went on a cold, forty degree day in March. His hands were frozen by the time he arrived home. I had to unzip his jacket and take his gloves off and help warm up his hands. It took a lot of effort to keep from saying, "I told you it was too cold to do this today."

The motorcycle memory that stands out the most is when Matt took me to a Michael W. Smith concert on the motorcycle. We enjoyed the concert and spending time with our good friends Ted and Audrey. As we were walking toward the parking lot, it started to rain and hail. It was coming down so hard and fast that it hurt. Everyone ran to their cars. I was extremely relieved when Matt recommended that Ted and Audrey drive me home. Matt put on his rain gear and managed to get home safe but soaking wet. A lesson was learned to check the weather reports before venturing out on his bike.

Ted and Audrey were another huge answer to prayer regarding friends. We loved getting together with them for game nights. We shared about what God was doing in our lives. We encouraged them and likewise, they encouraged us. We also challenged each other regarding spiritual and theological issues.

Life was going along smoothly until August of 2001, when Matt was one of four hundred employees who were laid off. We were suddenly in a scary scenario. All of our savings had gone into our new home and car so there was no extra money to tap into. Fortunately, Matt received an excellent severance package and we had full health care coverage and full pay for six months. We were extremely confident that Matt could find a new job right away and we would be financially ahead.

During those six months Matt sent out hundreds of resumes, drove to several businesses, prayed, and did all he could think of to find a decent job. There were many times when we were enthusiastic about a job thinking that it was the perfect fit for Matt. We would say, "Yes, this must be it. This is the job we have been praying and waiting for. Okay, God. We understand Your plan. This is the door You are opening." Only to have that door quickly slammed in our face. We went through this cycle time and time again.

Several times I walked into the room and found Matt on his knees crying out to God. It was a beautiful sight to see my husband humbled before the Lord but it also saddened me to see Matt so broken. I was used to Matt being strong. This was a new side of him and I didn't know how to handle it. I cried out to God to send Matt a great job. My solution was a great job and so I didn't realize at the time all the lessons God was teaching us in the waiting.

After five fabulous years, my babysitting job came to an end. I missed JD and Megan terribly but enjoyed the flexibility of taking Eric to his therapy classes twice a week. Eric had some developmental delays and was in need of physical, occupational, and speech therapy. He was in a classroom setting with three other two-year-olds. I enjoyed talking with the other moms and was grateful to his teacher for her dedication.

Before we knew it, it was January 2002 and our precious Jeremy Alan was born by Cesarean section. What a blessing to have a healthy baby, something we did not take for granted. I was thrilled to be able to hold him and nurse him right away. Friends and family gathered around the hospital bed to meet Jeremy. My parents had recently moved back to Michigan and we were thankful for their help. Matt's parents also came to help out for a week which was greatly appreciated as well. We were grateful for this joyful birth amidst the uncertainty of our financial situation.

However, God continued to provide for us – in His own way. Matt's severance pay and health insurance coverage expired the day after we brought Jeremy home from the hospital. God's perfect timing, indeed! To say that money was getting very tight is an understatement. What a humbling time in life this was. We had to ask family to help us out with our mortgage payment. People from church gave us gift cards, money, and groceries. Matt and I were extremely grateful and felt blessed to be supported in this way.

Here was another big test in trusting God. Driving to church one Sunday, God gave me a very specific amount to put in the offering. It was more than I felt comfortable giving but I was obedient. As we were leaving church, someone handed us a gift card to a grocery store in the exact amount I had put in the offering. As I was thanking God for His provision, I was reminded of Malachi 3:10, *"Bring the whole tithe into the storehouse, that there may be food in my house. Test me in this,"* says the Lord Almighty, *"and see if I will not throw open the floodgates of heaven and pour out so much blessing that you will not have room enough for it."*

I started to feel guilty. I had not been faithful in tithing during our time of financial growth and here we were receiving blessing. In the past I had given God our leftovers instead of our first and best. Now that we were in this time of financial devastation, God lovingly provided. He also spoke some tough words to me. I needed to stop using Matt's spending as my reason for not giving to God. Matt may have been in disobedience regarding his spending, but I was also in disobedience for not tithing. He also pointed out how I had used our savings and Matt's job as my sense of financial security instead of trusting God.

Obviously, we are called to be good stewards with what God has given us and we need to be responsible and save money for the future and emergencies. My point is that we need to be open to letting God use our money and everything we have however He chooses. We can't pretend with God. He knows our heart. We had not given God complete access into our bank accounts. We had not allowed Him to truly be Lord over our money.

Shortly after Jeremy was born, Matt was hired into a company. Unfortunately he was not employed at his skill level or at his earning potential. This was in no way the big answer to our prayers that we were hoping for. It was difficult to make ends meet with our household income cut in half. Our income level bordered on the poverty level for a family of four. I am in no way comparing our situation to a family living in poverty. We were living in a brand new, beautiful home in a nice subdivision. We never went hungry. It just became a struggle to pay our monthly bills.

When Jeremy was just a few weeks old, Matt told me he wanted to rejoin the National Guard. I started crying and begged him not to. I did not want to deal with any more separations especially now that we had children. Also, I did not want to live with the fear of Matt being in harm's way. This was shortly after September 11, 2001 and we were still hurting along with the nation over that tragic day. I told him I would get a full-time job. Despite my protest, he rejoined the National Guard in hopes that this would bring more job opportunities. Over time, my attitude changed to that of gratefulness. I was proud of Matt for being so determined to support both his family and his country.

We both came to the conclusion that it would be easier for me to find a job in my field. My degree was in Family Life Education. Matt helped me update my resume as he had become an expert on writing resumes and applying for jobs. The thought of having to leave my infant and toddler and go to work was heartbreaking. Ever since childhood I had a deep desire to be home with my children. Why was it being taken away from me? I was angry with God. I was angry with my husband. I was angry with the economy. I was angry with the terrorists.

It will come as no surprise when I admit that I was happy when I did not get any job offers. But it broke my heart as I watched my husband sink into a deeper depression. I kept saying, "Of course you're depressed. Who wouldn't be in this situation?" Matt was so ambitious. He was so intelligent. He wanted so desperately to be working in a challenging, adequately paid environment. I was getting burnt out from playing the cheerleader role.

Our trust in God was being put to the test and we wanted to remain full of hope but the hope was starting to fade. Our prayers started to sound like this: "*Okay God, what are you doing here? How much longer is this going to go on? We don't see your plan in this.*

Your timing is obviously way different from our timing. Where are you, God? Why are no doors opening?" I wasn't hearing much from God during this time. Perhaps I was still too focused on "a good job" as our solution instead of giving God complete control and trusting Him to be our perfect solution. I was thinking of human answers instead of God answers. Why do we limit God like that?

Laughter is good medicine. I will always treasure a two-minute reprieve we had from all our stress. Why is it that babies always seem to cry at mealtime? Matt and I had just sat down to eat a nice, hot dinner when Jeremy started crying. It was a hunger cry. Eric also wanted to make his presence known so he began crying and pouting so that we would give him some attention. Or maybe he was crying because he didn't like the meal I had prepared. Either way, both kids were crying quite loudly. Matt got up from the table, took my hand and asked me to dance with him. He said, "This is the music God gave us, we are going to dance to it." We laughed and enjoyed a minute or two of dancing and then resumed our parental responsibility of tending to our crying children.

CHAPTER 6

Hoping for Change

Winter turned to spring and with it came times of rejoicing. On June 5, 2002 Matt and I celebrated our ten year wedding anniversary. My mom babysat and gave us a gift certificate to one of our favorite restaurants. Three days later Matt graduated with a Master of Science in Computer Information Systems. We had a small party at our house with family.

Have you ever had one of those moments where you think, *Why didn't anyone tell me I looked like that?* Here is one such time and this is not an exaggeration. Looking at the pictures from Matt's graduation, I clearly look five months pregnant instead of looking like the mom of an almost five-month-old. The only dress that fit me at the time was one of those long, loose-fitting jumpers. When I was skinny, it fit right. However, in these pictures it was a very tight fit and revealed my large, post-pregnant stomach. I can, sort of, laugh about it now.

Later that month, we enjoyed three days of fun with the entire Matzinger family celebrating Rex and Dorothy's 50th wedding anniversary. It was the first time all eleven of the grandchildren had been together and my first time meeting four of my nieces and nephews. Dorothy, Matt's mom, wanted to wear a white dress because she could not wear white when they got married. Dorothy was widowed at the age of 21 and she married Rex four years later. Back in 1952, it was not socially acceptable to wear white for a second marriage.

Matt's sisters: Kathleen, Ellen Marie, Joanna, and Carolyn were doing cheers from their high school days at Romeo High. Ellen Marie's idea for the immediate family to write "The Matzinger Memories" was a big hit. I had spent six months creating a scrapbook and each of their five children read from the page, "Mother Sew Dear" as mom liked to sew and "Dad Gets Our Stamp of Approval." Dad collected stamps. The entire weekend was a blast.

It felt refreshing to laugh because we had been crying just a few weeks earlier when we had to put our five year old Labrador retriever, Jasmine, to sleep. Matt and I comforted each other right before he walked Jasmine out of the house for the last time. I never had a pet growing up so this was my first experience dealing with the death of a pet. The house felt so empty with Jasmine gone. Our poor Simba had lost his playmate. Weeks later he was still moping around the house looking for Jasmine. Eric was three years old and Jeremy was only a few months old so they didn't seem bothered by it.

As the fall winds blew, we encountered more changes. Matt's National Guard Unit was put on Homeland Security at a local air force base. We were all thankful he was stationed locally. Matt enjoyed his mission and was proud to be serving his country. I was proud of him as well and happy for him that he liked his job.

Money was still tight and so I jumped at the opportunity to babysit for a friend of a friend. Through this new family another part-time job opened up for me at their church. My dear mother, who lived forty-five minutes away, drove to our house three days a week so that I could go to work and not pay for childcare. My mom is an incredible lady and Matt and I greatly appreciated her. She was always there for me when I needed her. Throughout my life she had been a wonderful example of what sacrificial love is. "*Thank you, God, for my mother. Please bless her for her dedication, obedience, and willingness to serve.*"

It was sometime during this time frame that I committed to reading through the Bible in a year. It was something I had always wanted to do and what better time than now. I followed the plan of a one-year Bible which had me reading verses from the Old Testament, the New Testament and a Psalm and a Proverb every day. It took a year and a half for me to complete all the readings. The more I was in the Word, the more I realized how much I needed to be in God's Word and wanted to be in the Word every day. It was a time of spiritual growth for me.

I found God's Word to be comforting and full of hope. Proverbs 3:5 gave me hope. "*Trust in the Lord with all your heart and lean not on your own understanding; in all your ways acknowledge him, and he will make your paths straight.*" I had no idea what lay ahead for Matt and I or how much longer Matt would be under worked and under paid but I was going to trust God.

I clung to the words of Jeremiah 29:11-13: "*For I know the plans I have for you," declares the Lord, "plans to prosper you and not to harm you, plans to give you hope and a future. Then you will call upon me and come and pray to me, and I will listen to you. You will seek me and find me when you seek me with all your heart.*" I cried out to God, "I'm seeking you Lord. I'm seeking you." I did find comfort knowing that God knew the plans He had for us; but I longed for God to tell us what those plans were.

Also in Jeremiah I had read several times and highlighted chapter 32:17: *"Ah, Sovereign Lord you have made the heavens and the earth by your great power and outstretched arm. Nothing is too hard for you."* Nothing is too hard for God. Nothing! God could easily open up a door of great opportunity for Matt even in this tough Michigan economy. Our job was to wait patiently.

Another verse that was full of hope was Joshua 23:14: *"You know with all your heart and soul that not one of all the good promises the Lord your God gave you has failed. Every promise has been fulfilled; not one has failed."* I knew I could trust God but I had to admit that many times fear had prevented me from fully being able to trust Him.

In Philippians 4:19, I read *"And my God will meet all your needs according to his glorious riches in Christ Jesus."* I repeated that verse over and over again as well as Psalm 23:1 *"The Lord is my shepherd, I shall not be in want."*

The joy that 1 John 3:1a brought me every time I read it: *"How great is the love the Father has lavished on us, that we should be called children of God!"* I am God's child and he loves me more than I can comprehend. God saw our situation. God knew what we needed. God loved us with an unfailing love. Knowing I was loved by God gave me hope.

Another big spiritual step for us was switching denominations. We visited a local Non-Denominational church because we couldn't make it on time to our Lutheran church. We felt God calling us to go back there again and again. Eventually, we took the membership class and felt God's peace regarding our new church home. As you can guess, that didn't go over so well with our families who were long-standing Lutherans.

I loved this time in my spiritual journey. What an opportunity for growth. I asked a lot of questions and a lot of questions were asked of me. I was digging deep into the Bible for answers and asking God for discernment. I asked myself this question numerous times, "Do I believe this or that because it is what I was taught or do I believe it because that is what the Bible says?"

My past judgments and my prejudices toward all non-Lutherans were lifted. I once thought that the Lutherans had it all right and that everyone else was a little bit off. Now I see the world through different eyes. The important issue isn't whether you are Lutheran, Baptist, Methodist, Presbyterian, Non-Denominational, or the like, but whether you are saved or unsaved. People are either in the kingdom of God or they are not. There is nothing in-between. As believers, we need to focus our energy on reaching the unsaved instead of arguing with our fellow believers from different denominations. We need to mourn, hurt and pray fervently for those outside of God's family.

This reminds me of a story that Matt's friend told us back in our college days. When talking to his non-believing friends he would say, *"Okay, I want you to think about this. If I am wrong and you are right and there is no God then what do I lose? I still get to live my whole life with the hope of Jesus and the resurrection. Furthermore, I get to draw strength from God in my day-to-day living. If there is no eternal life then I won't even know I was wrong. I will just die and that will be the end of me. However, if I am right which I believe with all my heart that I am, and you are wrong then what happens to you? You spend your whole earthly life without the daily comfort of knowing who God is and knowing His amazing love for you. And then when you die, you will spend an eternity in hell. Are you sure you don't want to get to know Jesus?"*

Jesus is the only way to heaven. We can't earn our salvation. No one can ever be good enough to get into heaven. It is a free gift given to us because of God's great love for us. Jesus said these words found in John 14:1-6: "*Do not let your hearts be troubled. Trust in God; trust also in me. In my Father's house are many rooms; if it were not so, I would have told you. I am going there to prepare a place for you. And if I go and prepare a place for you, I will come back and take you to be with me that you also may be where I am. You know the way to the place where I am going.*" *Thomas said to him,* "*Lord, we don't know where you are going, so how can we know the way?*" *Jesus answered,* "*I am the way and the truth and the life. No one comes to the Father except through me.*"

I will remain a student of God's Word for the rest of my life. Matt and I wanted to be in a Bible study. Our neighbors down the street attended the same church and they invited us to join their small group. We studied Rick Warren's book, *A Purpose Driven Life*. What a great time in life to be reading this book. I needed this reminder that life was about God and not about me. I realized that I was not truly living a completely surrendered life. I was still living with the hope that God would bless my plans instead of asking God what plans He had for me.

Choosing to stay focused on the character of God and not on my circumstances was a difficult task during this time of uncertainty. Even with the four jobs between us, we still weren't making the amount of money our budget needed. The financial burden was weighing us down. We needed a change. We prayed for a change. Does "be careful what you pray for" come to mind?

The summer of 2004 brought about a big change geographically as well as a big change spiritually. I was given another opportunity to trust God with Eric's life. This opportunity came about as we were celebrating my dad's retirement. Technically, my dad was not fully retiring. He was changing from full-time to part-time pastor which meant instead of working sixty hours a week he would work about thirty. My three siblings and I had all planned speeches to give at the fabulous party that the church gave for my dad.

Right before I was supposed to talk, one of the employees at the banquet hall told me that I had an emergency phone call. I remember saying, "Can't it wait? I am about to speak."

"You need to come with me now!" she insisted. Matt had just left to get home to the boys because our babysitters had somewhere they needed to be. I reasoned that it must be Matt calling.

"This is Karen," I said.

"This is your neighbor behind you," a male voice answered. "There are several emergency vehicles at your house. One of your sons was stung by a bee and is having a severe allergic reaction. The ambulance is in route to the nearest hospital."

I called Matt's cell phone. He had just listened to the several messages on his phone so he was already headed to the hospital. Of all the days, we had left Matt's cell phone in the car while we were at the retirement party so we had no idea that the babysitters were frantically trying to get a hold of us.

I prayed for Eric and then went back into the party room to give my speech. I had to trust God. God had gotten Eric through open heart surgery at the tender age of four days old. Surely He could keep Eric safe after a bee sting. Somehow I just knew that Eric was going to be okay. It hadn't yet hit me that Eric had gone into anaphylactic shock. I would later find out that Eric's throat was rapidly swelling making it difficult to breathe and that his very life was being threatened. I wasn't with Eric at that moment but I knew God was. That alone brought me comfort and hope.

I was determined to make sure my parents heard my accolades. I opened my speech with "One of the main reasons my dad was able to be such a great pastor and dad was because he had my mom by his side." I wanted to make sure my mom received recognition so I read a poem that I had written for her.

A Tribute to My Mom

It has been said that the wife and mother is the heart of the home.
And you mom are the best as you will hear in this poem.
Motherhood is hard but you made it look so easy and fun.
We never realized how tired you must have been when the day was done.
Having four children our needs came ahead of your own.
You always gave cheerfully we never once heard you moan.
You kept busy cooking, cleaning, laundry, and there was lots to dust.
When you asked us to help we are sorry we put up such a fuss.
For being a stay-at-home mom we thank you so very much,
For there is nothing more comforting than a mother's loving touch.
For being a kind, fun, creative and happy mom we thank you.
For we felt safe and secure, happy and content each day as we grew.
You are still and will always be a wonderful, loving Christian mother.
And I thank you for giving me two kind sisters and one great brother.
I wish everyone could have experienced the loving home I had.
And you deserve a gold medal for putting up with dear old dad.
You made it clear church activities were important to do.
You volunteered for VBS and remained active in Bible study too.
You enjoyed your time with the ladies as the bells you were ringing.
And your smiling face was a joy as in the choir you were singing.
It is evident that being a grandma is a joy and a fun-loving task.
You come over to babysit whenever Jennifer or I ask.
I can't thank you enough for everything you continue to do.
I hope that someday I can be as great a mom as you.
You are the perfect example of a pastor's wife.
And you should be proud to have led a Proverbs 31 life.
These appropriate verses I now share with you.
It does not rhyme but the words are certainly true.

She is clothed with strength and dignity; she can laugh at the days to come. She speaks with wisdom, and faithful instruction is on her tongue. She watches over the affairs of her household and does not eat the bread of idleness. Her children arise and call her blessed; her husband also, and he praises her: "Many women do noble things, but you surpass them all." (Proverbs 31:25-29)

Immediately upon finishing my poem I tearfully announced that I had to get to the hospital to see my son. Pastor Mike came running up to the microphone and said, "We need to pray right now." My family all ran up to hug me as Pastor Mike prayed. All of a sudden the seriousness of Eric's situation hit me.

My Uncle John drove me to the hospital and his presence was comforting to me. He was currently employed as a hospital chaplain. I remember praying the whole twenty-minute drive there. "Please God let Eric be alive when I get there."

Matt was about fifteen minutes ahead of me and pulled into the parking lot at the same time as the ambulance. He was with Eric until I could get there. I ran in and saw that Eric was okay.

"Thank you God!" Our sensational, responsible babysitters had done the right thing and called 911 just in time. How could we ever thank Ashley and Christina enough? What amount of pay could we possibly give them for saving our son's life? We paid them as generously as we could afford to.

Next came the geographical change. Matt continued to research jobs and found a great job through the National Guard working on computers with the Missile Defense Agency. This sounded like Matt's dream job. There was one catch, the job was in Alaska. We prayed and prayed and prayed some more. *"What do we do, God? Are we doing this because we don't trust You to provide a job here in Michigan? Are we supposed to stay and wait this out? Is this the job you are providing and we would be foolish not to take it?"* We truly sought out God's direction and guidance. After lots of prayer, we both felt at peace with the decision to move to Alaska.

Within the same week of Matt getting the Alaska job, we found out that I was pregnant. We were very excited as we had both wanted three children. The "For Sale" sign went up and I tried my best to keep the house clean and presentable. Eric was five years old and Jeremy was two, so toys were scattered throughout the house.

I was physically tired being that it was my first trimester. There were times when we only had a thirty-minute notice that a realtor was coming by to show the house. I remember running around the house cleaning and picking up after the boys which seemed to be a lost cause. One time we had left the house in a hurry and we had left it a complete mess. When we arrived home we saw a realtor's business card on our kitchen counter and we laughed as we realized someone had been looking at our house while we were gone. We were not surprised to learn that they did not want to buy the house.

As we pulled out of our driveway for the last time, we remained full of hope that our house would sell quickly. Why did we seem to keep having so many dramatic events in our life? Matt and I began praying for some uneventful years. There wasn't much time to catch our breath before our next adventure. Matt and I wondered if Alaska was where we would find our mountain of hope.

CHAPTER 7

SEARCHING FOR OUR MOUNTAIN OF HOPE

We were on our way to Alaska! I kept a journal and wrote a poem about our adventures.

Our Journey Northwest

It is an exciting time as I begin a new chapter in my life.
I'm sure I will have plenty more as I am once again a military wife.
But before each new journey begins, the old one sadly must end.
It was very difficult to say goodbye to my family and my friends.

The emotions ran high as I cleaned one last time our house on Clear Lake.
All offers from neighbors and family to help I gladly did take.
So a huge "thank you" to Amy, Charlotte, Jennifer, and Jessica I do say.
And to Grandma Burow whose house Eric and Jeremy could play.

I have many happy memories and I will miss you all so very much.
But I know with phone calls, e-mails, and yearly visits we will always
*   keep in touch.*
And now I take you with me as I share the details of our exciting journey.
Our van is full with barely enough room for Matt and I, Simba, Eric,
*   and Jeremy.*

Our first stop was to Wisconsin to see some of the Burow Family.
We wish our stay could have been longer as we always enjoy their
    hospitality.
We crossed the Mississippi and drove to Rochester, Minnesota where we
    spent the night.
Driving through the farmlands was probably our most boring sight.

We made it to South Dakota where the speed limit is 75 — Hurray!
We drove past the home of Laura Ingalls Wilder that day.
We crossed the Missouri River and entered the Mountain Time Zone.
The badlands were so spectacular they could only have been formed by
    God alone.

And what a thrill it was to see a national monument — Mount Rushmore.
Then headed to Gillette, Wyoming for lunch as our stomachs started to roar.
Driving through Montana we were surrounded by mountain ranges.
It was such a beautiful sight to see all the fall color changes.
Who could forget Eric's quote of the day as he did sing.
"God is so awesome. He makes really awesome things!"

But Oregon wins for the most breathtaking state.
Driving the National Columbia River Gorge was truly 1st rate.
We called Aunt Betty to say we were in The Dalles which she couldn't
    believe.
We had dinner with the rest of their family where we were so warmly
    received.

Then on to Battleground, Washington to see our good friends.
The Petersons were so much fun we didn't want it to end.
Even Simba had a doggy friend to play with there.
And Kyle and Tyler did great with all the toys they had to share.

The ferry boat was definitely another major highlight.
The Alaska Marine highway was quite a spectacular sight.
We were in some rough waters and we felt a little seasick.
There was so much to do, but it was the play area that the boys usually
*   did pick.*

We have finally arrived in Fairbanks – our final destination.
God deserves all the glory and praise for His beautiful creation.
Alaska is a most majestic, incredible, breathtaking, yet far away land.
We are at peace knowing we are in God's loving yet powerful and
*   mighty hands.*

You may ask if we have any regrets about our decision to drive.
No way! How else could we have seen this amazing countryside?
We thank our God that He kept us safe on our amazing trip so long.
We leave you with the words to this most popular song.
"From the mountains to the prairies, to the oceans white with foam.
God bless America, My home sweet home."
And God bless Fairbanks, my NEW sweet home.

October had always been my favorite month. I loved the beauty of the color change we see throughout Michigan. October in Fairbanks meant snow on the ground. We went from wearing shorts in the lower forty-eight states to wearing snow gear in Fairbanks. I felt homesick for Michigan. We had to spend ten days living in a regular hotel room because there were no openings at the Army hotel.

I knew no one in Alaska yet. Matt was working one hundred miles away so he could not even come home every day. I was stuck in a small hotel room with two young, active boys and a 90 pound dog. The hotel management said I could not leave our dog in the room alone so every time we went out, I had to bring Simba with us. We had a microwave and mini fridge in the room so we had pretty basic meals.

It felt like luxury when we could move into the Army hotel. Matt and I had an actual bedroom. The boys slept on the pull-out sofa in the living room and we had a decently stocked kitchen with a stove. No more having to eat on the floor or on the beds because we now had a table and four chairs. Plus we received a free continental breakfast every day. The boys loved going to the lobby to pick out their mini cereal box and muffin every morning.

The Army had the same rule regarding dogs as the other hotel. Every time I left the room I had to take Simba with me. I wasn't even allowed to bring him through the front door. I had to use the back door which led out to a yard that was covered with a foot of snow. Walking all around the building in deep snow in temperatures below zero with two young children and a dog was wearisome on my expanding pregnant body.

I would be in tears and the boys were nearly frozen by the time we reached the parking lot. I tend to be a rule follower but this was getting ridiculous. Time to put Plan B into motion which was to leave Simba in our room and put the 'Do Not Disturb' sign on the door so that housekeeping wouldn't come in and discover our big violation. All I wanted was to be able to walk out the front door with my children. We did get caught but housekeeping took pity on us and let us continue to leave Simba in the room.

This hotel living was getting old. The boys and I were by ourselves most of the time because Matt was working one hundred miles from Fairbanks. The Army hired Matt under the stipulation that we would live in Fairbanks in order to be close to a hospital due to Eric's heart condition. Matt would come "home" once during the week. The other nights he would stay in the barracks near his job. After three weeks of traveling back and forth on the snowy, icy roads and living away from us, both the Army and Matt realized this was not going to work. Matt requested a transfer and it was granted within a week.

Matt would often ask me, "What do you want first, the good news or the bad news?" I wasn't quite sure how to respond when he arrived back at our hotel with that question. He continued saying, "The good news is that I will be working in downtown Fairbanks. The bad news is that I am back to doing very unchallenging work."

I immediately questioned God, "Why would You move us all the way up here only to have Matt give up his dream job within a few weeks of living in Alaska? This makes no sense." Immediately God gave me a peace about it all even though I couldn't understand why this was happening.

Our next good news/bad news came a week later. Our wonderful realtor back in Michigan called saying, "You have an offer on your house. Unfortunately the offer is pretty low."

We prayed about it. Then Matt and I looked over the numbers and realized we could not afford to gamble and wait for another offer. Our neighbors and realtor were keeping an eye on our house for us and we felt it unfair to ask them to continue with that responsibility so we accepted the offer. At least we were able to walk away with a little bit of a profit.

Matt looked completely stressed out and depressed. He was carrying a heavy load feeling responsible for bringing us up to Alaska for what now seemed like a total waste. He was very unhappy and unfulfilled at his job working in supply. I did my best trying to keep up the encouragement and support. Some days I clung to the hope of knowing that we were here in Alaska for a reason. Other days I was questioning myself as to whether I was hearing God correctly.

One of the things we loved about Fairbanks was our church. We loved both of the pastors at Zion Lutheran Church. For the first time in my life I claimed Monday as my favorite day of the week. It was the day of the Mom's Bible Study and it was a very small group. The other moms quickly became my best friends. After Bible study Matt would come have lunch with Jeremy and me. He worked five minutes from church so it was very convenient.

The boys seemed to be adjusting well. Eric really liked his school on the military base. The children played outside for recess unless it was colder than minus twenty degrees Fahrenheit. We also found it entertaining that the school had moose alerts. If a moose was spotted near the playground, the whistle would blow and the children would have to go inside immediately.

Jeremy and I were able to volunteer in Eric's kindergarten classroom one day a week. I was impressed with his teacher and really enjoyed seeing how she handled the students. Jeremy and I also attended a MOPS (Mothers of Preschoolers) group and we both looked forward to going twice a month. It was a different MOPS experience this time since I was not part of the steering team. I didn't feel as connected to the group but it was nice to be able to just show up and relax. Jeremy loved being in Moppets and wished he could have gone every day.

We also attended Romp-in-Stomp twice a week on Fort Wainwright. This was an indoor playgroup where Jeremy could play in a large room with other children and plenty of toys. One room contained slides, scooters, and other things that stimulated active play. The same few families came each week so I looked forward to talking with the other parents while

Jeremy played. This playgroup made the long, cold winter much more tolerable. In December and January we only had about four hours of daylight and the temperature was below zero.

After five weeks at the Army Hotel, we had reached our maximum allotted stay. We moved into a two bedroom furnished apartment in town as we were still waiting to get in to base housing. Laundry had been one of my favorite chores until now. The laundry facilities were located across the parking lot that never seemed to be plowed.

At this point in time my belly was so large that I could no longer zip up my coat. The average daily temperature was minus ten to minus thirty degrees. I took as much laundry as I could possibly carry and walked in knee high snow. There seemed to be a theme of me walking in deep snow. Perhaps I should have asked for snowshoes for Christmas.

In January we decided to rent a house off base instead of waiting for base housing. My favorite part about the house was that the laundry was located right across from the bedrooms. The boys loved the fact that we had a sledding hill in our yard. Matt loved living in a wooded area and being isolated from neighbors. We all were very excited to see our belongings that had been stored away for three months.

On January 3rd our long-awaited answer in regards to moving to Alaska came. Here is an e-mail I had sent out that day.

> *Dear Family,*
>
> *Just got word from Matt's good friend from his Michigan National Guard Unit in Lapeer. They just received orders to go to Iraq. If we were still living in Michigan, Matt would be going. Can you believe the timing? I love Alaska so much right now. I just can't stop thinking that if we were still in Michigan Matt would be missing the birth of our baby and probably missing the whole first year of the baby's life. Thank you God for sending us to Alaska!!!! All our doubts about coming here have just been put to rest. Please join us in saying a prayer of thanks for us. Then please say a prayer for our friend Gary and all those deployed to Iraq.*
>
> *Love, Matt and Karen*

There certainly didn't seem to be many dull moments in the Matzinger home. On March 9th my mom arrived in Fairbanks. Two days later we welcomed Keith Ethan into our family. He was a healthy 7 pound 4 ounce baby. I shared a room with two other moms at the Army hospital and Keith won the prize for the loudest and longest crier. The nurse on duty offered to take all three babies to the nursery during the night so we could get some sleep. I love nurses! My mom was impressed and very thankful that it was warmer in Alaska than it was back in Michigan. It was a sunny, forty degree day when Keith came home from the hospital.

Matt and I were extremely thankful for my mom's help. The day after Keith and I came home from the hospital I got the flu. I was miserable from the flu and sore from my C-section so I couldn't do much except feed Keith. My mom entertained the boys, cooked all the meals, did the laundry, and provided a calming presence in our home.

The two weeks with my mom flew by and before we knew it she was on her way back to Michigan. One week later Matt's parents arrived for their two week visit. It turned out to be a tough visit on me. Although I was physically feeling much better, I was struggling emotionally and not up to hosting anyone. I was homesick for Michigan and wished that all of our family could meet our darling little Keith. I was tense and took it out on Matt. Matt was very patient with me and very loving. The boys enjoyed the extra attention from grandpa and grandma. Matt took a few days off work to take his parents sightseeing. Keith and I enjoyed the peace and quiet.

Life with three boys kept us busy and entertained. We were discovering that Jeremy had inherited the Burow sense of humor and the Matzinger enthusiasm. He was constantly asking questions. I remember him pointing to a Bible and asking me, "What is that book? What does it say? Will you read it to me?"

I said to myself, "Relax. You know the Bible. You taught Sunday school and Vacation Bible School. You went to a Lutheran Elementary school and a Lutheran college. You can do this."

I felt a tremendous amount of pressure at that moment. I wanted my three year old Jeremy to not only know the Bible but to know Jesus. The verse that came to my mind was 1 Peter 3:15: "*But in your hearts set apart Christ as Lord. Always be prepared to give an answer to everyone who asks you to give the reason for the hope that you have. But do this with gentleness and respect.*" All along we had been teaching our children about Jesus and praying with them but this felt like a defining moment between God and Jeremy. "Please God, give me the right words."

"Jeremy, the Bible is about God's love for us and everything in the Bible is true. God loves you so much that He wants to spend forever with you. But there was a problem called sin. Sin is when you do not obey. Remember this morning when you didn't listen to me when I asked you to pick up your toys? That one sin is enough to keep you from going to heaven. But listen to this great news. God sent Jesus to die on a cross to take away all your sins. Jesus didn't stay dead. He became alive again. God wants you to place your complete trust and hope that Jesus is enough. You can never be good enough to earn your way into heaven. But it is okay because you don't have to be. Because of Jesus and only because of Jesus you get to go to heaven some day. The Bible says, "*That if you confess with your mouth, "Jesus is Lord," and believe in your heart that God raised him from the dead, you will be saved.*" (Romans 10:9)

Jeremy interrupted, "Okay mom. I get it. You can stop talking now."

Jeremy went back to playing and I thanked God for guiding me through this important conversation. Later that day I told Matt about our conversation and we prayed that all three of our boys would spend their lives getting to know Jesus better. Matt decided it was time to read a Bible verse at dinner every night and have the boys memorize it. Our wonderful friend had given us this idea.

Our helpful six-year-old Eric loved to shovel. Considering we had snow on the ground for six straight months, Alaska seemed a good fit for Eric. As the snow began melting in April, Eric discovered moose antlers right near our house. He was excited and it was definitely a Kodak moment. I was a bit nervous knowing that moose had been that close to our house.

There was actually a moose family living in our area and one day three moose decided to hang out by our front door. We watched moose instead of television that day. Eric was quite concerned about how dad was going to get inside our house. Eric made me call dad and warn him about the moose. The moose were at the front so dad came in the back door. Then Matt and Eric ventured outside to get a closer look. The moose heard them and took off into the woods. We still talk and laugh about that day.

Uncertain about how long we would be calling Alaska our home, we wanted to get some sightseeing in. Our activities were limited by three young boys but we still managed to see and do a lot. We made a special day out of watching the conclusion of the Yukon Quest. The Yukon Quest is a 1,000 mile sled dog race similar to the Iditarod. We were among those who lined up in Downtown Fairbanks to watch and wait for the racers to cross the finish line. Matt's boss gave him the afternoon off and we took Eric out of school early so we could see the winner. It was a true Alaska experience.

We only had to travel a few miles from home to see the Alaska Pipeline. After reading about it in history books, it was a thrill to be standing right underneath the pipes. Located twenty miles south of Fairbanks was North Pole, Alaska. Our Christmas photo that year was taken at the Santa Claus House in North Pole. The reindeer that lived there had very appropriate names. The boys kept looking for Rudolph. North Pole, Alaska also had a nice beach area where the boys and I went swimming in July.

As soon as all the roads were free of snow and ice, we drove two hours to Denali National Park with the hope of seeing Mt. McKinley, the largest peak in North America. We happened to go the day before the park officially opened so we did not have to pay an admission fee. Unfortunately, clouds were hiding Mt. McKinley. A month later we drove by Denali National Park on our way to Anchorage. This time we had the most incredible view of Mt. McKinley. Words cannot describe its beauty. Pictures cannot capture its magnificence. One can only gaze at its magnitude and be in complete awe of its Creator. It is a humbling, yet exhilarating experience.

Unfortunately, the boys were too young to appreciate the beauty of it all. According to Eric and Jeremy the highlight of our Anchorage trip was going to Chuck E. Cheese. They did enjoy being in Wasilla at the Iditarod Trail Race Headquarters. I have a cute picture of Jeremy petting one of the husky puppies. It was a breathtaking drive from Anchorage to Seward. I wanted to stop every two minutes to take a picture but I settled for postcards. We did stop when a baby moose fell off a cliff. The boys kept calling dad a hero because he called animal rescue.

Summer in Fairbanks brought long days and short nights. There were twenty-two hours of sunlight in June. We put heavy duty foil on the windows to keep our bedrooms dark so that we could fall asleep at night. When we went to bed at eleven o'clock at night, the sun was still out. The streets of Fairbanks were full of vacationers and tour buses. It was a thrill to participate in the Midnight Sun Run. My friend Karen and I walked all 6.2 miles along with hundreds of other walkers and runners. Some people went all out and entered the costume contest. There were walkers who dressed up as the statue of liberty, a bubble bath person, and lots of other interesting costumes. Despite the rain and clouds, there was still daylight at midnight when we reached the finish line. It was another amazing experience, unique to Alaska.

Summer was quickly coming to an end but not without another big announcement. On August 13, 2005 I sent out the following e-mail:

> *I write this with a sad and heavy heart. Matt has been ordered to go to Kuwait. He leaves for training in New Jersey sometime during September and then goes to Kuwait from there. Matt was hand-selected by the Battalion Commander for this special mission. Only ten soldiers from the entire battalion are going and Matt made the top ten list. This is a HUGE compliment to Matt but definitely not the kind of compliment we wanted. Matt does not want to leave us. He will be gone for over a year. Please cover him in prayer.*
>
> *The military will be moving the boys and me back to Michigan. I can hardly eat or sleep but am trying to function for the sake of the boys. Matt is currently on annual training so we haven't even had time together since this news. I really don't have more details at this time so please just say a prayer instead of e-mailing back with questions.*
>
> *Trusting in the Lord now more than ever, Karen*

I wish I could say that I was truly trusting in God and feeling His peace but I had several worrisome moments. My stomach was upset due to worry and anger. My prayers were questions to God. "Why? This makes no sense. Remember several months ago, God, when you told me that we were in Alaska to keep Matt from going overseas? What happened to that plan? Don't You see Matt falling into a deeper depression? Why would You make us go through another long separation when we need each other so much right now?"

Needing to hear a rational voice, I called our pastor. I shared the news with him and started crying. "Pastor Jonathan, this may sound crazy but I keep seeing Matt's funeral in the near future. If he goes to Iraq, he won't come home alive. I can feel it. God has given me a clear vision of Matt's funeral. I can't get it out of my head. You are preaching at it."

Pastor responded with, "Okay, maybe you need to plan Matt's funeral. Maybe that will help you feel at ease."

I had no idea that in exactly eight months from that moment, Pastor Jonathan really would be preaching at Matt's funeral.

When Matt came home from his two weeks of annual training, we held each other for a very long time. We were both exhausted from all the ups and downs of the past several years. Looking into each other's eyes, our silence seemed to say, "Why do we keep facing so many extremes? What are we doing wrong? Perhaps we need to change our prayers and make them more specific. I love you Honey. God will get us through this. We must remain full of hope that God has a plan for us."

Matt added, "Karen, you know I don't want to leave you and the boys but if I'm supposed to go to Iraq, then I will go."

I said, "I know. I wouldn't expect any less from you."

I sent an e-mail on Friday, September 2, 2005.

> *Hello Friends,*
>
> *Here is an incredible answer to prayer! Matt and I have been praying specifically that God would soften the commander's heart and remove Matt from the list since there are so many soldiers who were begging to go to Iraq. Well the list went from 10 soldiers to 70 soldiers and*

miraculously Matt's name was taken off the list. Even Matt's boss said, "You must have been praying because there is no other way to explain your name being removed from the list." Yes, this was totally God at work.

Not only is Matt not going to Iraq, but paperwork is in the process of transferring Matt back to Michigan so we can be closer to Children's Hospital. Matt has an interview with the National Guard for a job near Battle Creek. He is also seriously looking at civilian jobs as well. In the meantime looks like we will be back in Michigan before the end of 2005. All five of us.

Give God all the glory. This truly is a miracle!

Thank you all for your prayers, encouraging e-mails, and cards. Very much appreciated!

We have so much to be thankful for. Our prayers at this time go to everyone dealing with the devastation of the hurricane. And also to our many friends who are serving overseas.

Love, Karen

A month later I found myself with more big news to share. I sent another e-mail on Wednesday, October 5, 2005.

Hi Friends,

Sorry for all the mass e-mails but it's just easier to type this message just once.

To keep this as short and simple as possible, the army is releasing Matt from active duty due to Eric's heart condition. Alaska cannot properly treat Eric if he should need surgery which puts Matt on non-deployable status. They never should have allowed us to be here in the first place. So the army is moving us back to Michigan but it's up to Matt to find a job. He did not get the Battle Creek National Guard job which is fine because he didn't want it anyway.

*The movers are coming to pack us up Oct. 12 - 14. We leave Fairbanks on the 16th to catch the ferry on the 17th. **Here's the real exciting part**. Matt is flying back to Michigan for a 2nd interview for a telecommunications job that he really wants in northern Michigan. Sooooo, the boys and I are going to drive from Fairbanks to Arcadia without Matt. Okay, I know what you're thinking. Don't panic! I can do this.*

Don't worry. Just pray and turn to Deut. 31:8. "The Lord himself goes before you and will be with you; he will never leave you nor forsake you. Do not be afraid; do not be discouraged."

Signing off from Alaska,
Karen

CHAPTER 8

HOPING FOR A JOB

Emotions were running high once again. I was thrilled beyond words to be moving back to Michigan. But I also did not want to say good-bye to my Bible study friends. What will I do without them? My Mondays will never be the same. The very best part about living in Fairbanks was being part of the church family at Zion Lutheran. I will miss helping Pastor Jonathan do the PowerPoint and I will miss Lenetta's Sunday morning class along with all the wonderful families that were in class with Matt and me.

In my final scrapbook page on Alaska I wrote: With tears I came to Alaska and it is with tears that I now leave Alaska. It may be the coldest state but it has the warmest people. What an adventure this past year has been... Overall Alaska was a good place for some special family time. Matt only had a 15-minute commute so he was home by 5:15 P.M. each evening. The slower pace-of-living made it easy to get together with friends on a short notice. Matt is flying back to Michigan for a job interview and I volunteered to drive back with all three boys. There was no guarantee that Matt will get this job but I wanted him to have the chance to at least interview for it. I am about to begin an adventure of a lifetime. Little did I know at the time that God was using this trip to prepare me for all that is yet to come.

My family was worried that I might get lost as I have known to be directionally challenged. I tried to put them at ease by saying, "All I have to do is drive south and east. Plus I just drove this exact route a year ago. I can do this. I need to do this for Matt. He passed the first interview by phone but the second interview needs to be done in person. They are making a hiring decision within the week so in order for Matt to be considered he must fly back to Michigan. I realize there is no guarantee that Matt will get this job but he needs this opportunity. Matt is already feeling down about the job situation. I have to do this for Matt."

The van was packed as full as possible, similar to our drive to Alaska. The difference was we didn't have Matt or Simba this time. Our beloved dog Simba died of leukemia back in May. We were still missing him and weren't ready for another dog. The second difference was that Keith was in the van. I was pregnant with him one year ago when we drove to Fairbanks. Keith was now seven months old, Jeremy was three and a half and Eric was six.

I truly was feeling confident at the beginning of the trip. My excitement of living near family overpowered my practical side. Matt kissed the boys and I goodbye and he promised he would pray for us. Matt gave me his cell phone because I didn't have one and told me to call him at least once a day. We prayed that God would be with us every mile of the journey and keep us safe.

The roads were snow covered and icy the day we left Fairbanks. However, I felt confident in my driving ability as I had one full year experience of driving on the Alaska roads. I was not happy to be stuck behind a slow-moving full size pick-up truck.

"Why is he driving so slowly? The road conditions aren't that bad," I grumbled.

I was quickly losing patience and I had only been on the road a half hour. As I applied my brakes, I realized that I was driving on black ice and immediately started thanking God for the truck in front of me that kept me from driving too fast.

My goal for the first day was to drive three hundred miles and spend the night in Beaver Creek, Yukon Territory, Canada. As I approached the Alaska/Canada border, I was stopped and questioned, "Where is the father of these children and why isn't he with you?"

Two nights before leaving Fairbanks, a friend had suggested that I have a notarized note from Matt giving me permission to cross the border with the children. I handed the note from Matt, all our birth certificates, and other important paperwork to the border patrol. He was satisfied and we were on our way. Without that note, I would have been sent back to Fairbanks and would have missed our ferry boat. *Thank you, God for the wisdom of our friend.*

As I drove through the mountains I was starting to have doubts about my brilliant plan of doing this without Matt's help. The cell phone did not work during this part of the trip and exits were one hundred miles apart. I was the only one on the road. Maybe once every hour a car would pass going in the opposite direction. It was time for Keith to be fed and there was no exit anywhere near me. I pulled over to the side of the road and left the van running for fear it would not start up again.

There wasn't much room in the van for me to hold Keith comfortably and feed him a bottle. My legs were bent in ways they were not meant to be bent but I managed to make it work. I was in constant communication with God throughout this trip and I felt His presence in the van with us. Just when I didn't think I could take one more look at the snowy mountains, I would round the corner just in time to see another spectacular view. There was freshly fallen snow on the shoulder of the road but the actual road was completely dry. Could this be another one of God's miracles?

One of my most memorable views was near Haines, Alaska. It was a beautiful fall day. The colorful leaves were a welcomed change from the snow. Above the fall colors were the beautiful evergreens and above that were the snow-covered mountains. Not even a postcard could capture the beauty that my eyes were privileged to see. We were also thrilled to observe dozens of bald eagles.

We arrived in Haines in plenty of time to catch our ferry boat. Getting checked in was the most stressful part of the whole trip. Keith was very fussy because we had just spent one hour in the van waiting to board. He was also hungry and tired. Once we were safely parked on the lower deck, the boys and I went upstairs to get the key for our tiny cabin. I cried, *"How am I going to carry up everything we need from the van and what do I do with the boys?"* I had no choice but to leave the boys locked in the cabin while I ran downstairs to the car deck to bring up our luggage, the pack-n-play, the bag of food and formula, and toys for the boys. I ended up having to make two trips.

As soon as the boys were safely tucked in bed, I quickly unpacked and washed Keith's bottles. As soon as my head reached the pillow, I was asleep due to exhaustion. Now I can relax for three days and nights and enjoy the break from driving. We met several other families on the ferry boat. We ate our meals in the cafeteria. There was no way I could carry two trays of food plus push Keith's stroller, so I was very appreciative of my fellow passengers who came to my aid. The boat had a game/puzzle room, an observation deck, a mini theater, a gift shop, cabins, and other rooms but we spent most of the day in the play area.

By the time we arrived in Bellingham, Washington I felt refreshed and ready to hit the road again. It was a four hour drive to Battleground, Washington where we spent the night with our good friends, the Petersons. The kids had so much fun playing together and I enjoyed adult conversation, catching up on laundry, and the sunny, warm weather. Eric and Jeremy were wearing shorts. It was a welcomed change from snow pants. We then headed south to Oregon where we ate lunch with Aunt Betty and Uncle Maury.

The drive through Idaho's panhandle was absolutely beautiful! Traveling cross country with three young boys is not as stressful as one might think. They have been very well behaved in the car. Driving is the easy part. It is the rest stops and restaurants that were bothersome. There weren't any McDonald play places on our route through Montana and Wyoming. Being in the car all day, the boys didn't want to sit still in a restaurant and who can blame them?

We found a large facility complete with a gift shop and a restaurant. Using the bathroom with a seven-month-old, three-year-old, and six-year-old kept things interesting. As I was changing Keith's diaper Jeremy decided to peek under all ten bathroom stalls. Jeremy was out of my reach and I could not leave Keith lying on the changing table for fear of him rolling off. It was one of those moments where you wish your child would just listen to you the first time you called or even the third time. I can laugh about it now. At the time, I was praying that the other travelers would have sympathy on me and my situation.

It was a relief to make it to South Dakota and get a break from restaurants and hotels for the night. I was very excited to visit with my friend Heather. Heather and I had met in Fairbanks at MOPS. Her three boys were the exact same age as my three boys. Heather had moved back to South Dakota for the year her husband was deployed. She cooked a delicious dinner for us and the boys played together. After a great night of sleep, it was time to hit the road again. The boys cried when it was time to leave.

I was starting to feel worn out from this long road trip and was thankful that Minnesota was uneventful. We made it to Wisconsin and I have to admit I was exhausted. We were to spend a few days with Uncle Jim and Aunt Anita before reaching our final destination of Arcadia, Michigan. "Sorry Matt but you will have to wait a few extra days to see us."

Our time in Wisconsin was terrific and I felt refreshed. I was eager to drive the last 380 miles of this road trip and be reunited with Matt once again. We were extremely grateful for the wonderful hospitality of my sister Sarah and her husband Chip who lived in Arcadia. They allowed us to live in the upstairs part of their home which was comparable to a two-bedroom apartment. I was looking forward to getting lots of quality and quantity time with Sarah and Chip. An added bonus was that their daughter Grace was only three months younger than Keith.

When the boys and I arrived in Michigan, Matt wasn't there to greet us. When he walked in the door twenty minutes later, I was mad at first and cried, "Where were you? I can't believe you weren't home waiting for us! I was so anxious to see you that I made it home an hour early to surprise you."

Matt explained that he was out running errands and getting dinner for us. He was planning on having a hot dinner on the table for us when we arrived home. We had arrived home earlier than he was expecting so his surprise didn't work. He gave me that sweet grin of his and asked, "How about a hug?"

Then we each laughed about our surprise plan backfiring and we kissed and made up. The boys were thrilled to see daddy and told him all about our adventures. I loved having Matt wait on us and having all five of us together again under the same roof. I was hopeful that there wouldn't be any more separations of any kind.

Unfortunately, Matt did not get the job that he had flown back for. He heard these all too familiar words, "We felt one of the other candidates was a better fit for the job. Your resume and previous work experience are impressive and we wish we could have hired you as well." Feeling defeated and back at square one, Matt became more and more depressed. There were mornings when he did not want to get out of bed. However, Matt was not a quitter. He diligently continued on with the job search. There were a few strong possibilities which kept Matt somewhat optimistic. In the meantime he had found a temporary, entry level part-time job.

Spending Thanksgiving in Petoskey with the Matzinger family was a welcome change. The family surprised me with cards and a ribbon congratulating me on my successful cross country road trip. I remember saying, "I can do anything! I just drove from Alaska to Michigan with three young boys. Nothing sounds too hard right now."

I knew it was God who had protected us but at that moment I was taking full credit. Little did I know that three and a half months later my attitude about being able to do anything would drastically change.

In late January of 2006, a job offer in Matt's field finally came. I was thrilled! "Oh Matt, I'm so happy for you. This is exactly the kind of job we have been praying for since you were laid off back in 2001."

Matt didn't share my enthusiasm and I knew it was because of the depression. He said, "I have doubts about this job. I don't know if this is the right fit for me."

I questioned him. "Not the right fit? It is the perfect fit! Are you upset because this job is in Wisconsin and you were hoping to live and work in northern Michigan? Matt, this is a huge, long-awaited answer to prayer. What is going on?"

He replied, "I don't know. I can't explain it. Something about it just doesn't feel right. Let's pray about it, okay?"

We prayed about it and Matt accepted the job offer. He didn't want to but he knew it was the responsible thing to do. Matt reluctantly drove to Wisconsin and started the job mid-February. He was living with my aunt and uncle. We felt it best for the boys and me to remain in Arcadia so Eric could finish out the school year. Eric had already switched schools in October when we moved back from Alaska. Plus, it was one thing to ask for Matt to live with Uncle Jim and Aunt Anita but to ask for a family of five to live with them was a bit too much. They had a three bedroom home and my cousin Kim and her four-year-old son were also living with them.

It was difficult to be apart once again but we knew it was temporary. The day after Matt left for Wisconsin, Keith became quite ill. I ended up rushing him to the hospital because his breathing did not sound right. He was given breathing treatments and was diagnosed with pneumonia.

It was a very long, stressful week with Matt gone and Keith sick. Jeremy was bouncing off the walls in our little apartment. I remember telling Sarah, "I never, ever want to be a single mom. I don't know how single moms do it all. Matt has only been gone for a week and I don't know how I am going to make it three more months."

Matt wanted to be with us as much as we wanted to be with him. We were both burnt out from all the moving and all the challenges of the past few years. We were more than ready for life to calm down and just get back to the joy of day-to-day living. On a positive note, the challenges seemed to deepen our love for one another.

My Uncle Jim had a connection at the company where Matt was working. Matt's trainer and co-workers were very impressed with Matt and were looking forward to the positive changes Matt would be able to implement over time. They could tell right away how ambitious Matt was and how eager he was to learn. Matt was hired to write quality policies. Matt had years of experience in quality control and was extremely knowledgeable and capable of performing the tasks set before him. However, in talking to Matt each night, he sounded so unsure and so unhappy.

God put it on my heart to send Matt the following e-mail knowing that Matt's unhappiness was due to the depression and not the job:

Dear Matt,

    Just wanted to send you some encouraging words. I pray that you will keep a positive attitude regarding your job. God brought you to Wisconsin for a reason. Think of all the other doors that have closed. Ask God how you can best accomplish His purpose for your life during your time at this company. I pray that you will develop friendships with co-workers and that you will be patient because it takes time. I pray that your knowledge of quality is still fresh. I know you have a love for learning. I pray that you will find enjoyment, fulfillment, and satisfaction with your job and that your vision will be an asset to the company. You are a hard-working guy and I know you will give each day your all. I pray that you will be able to utilize your computer knowledge also. You have so much to offer. I pray that you can live your life with a more positive attitude and that you learn to make the best of your current circumstances. Matt, I have so much love and respect for you. You have stood the test of time during the past few years and you have come out the winner. I am really proud of you. I love you and I believe in you. Have a great day.
Love, Karen

I received the following e-mail from Matt on Valentine's Day:

Dear Sweetie,

    I thought I would write you this letter for Valentine's Day.

    I love you very much, and I realize as with how the current situation stands that I have been financially irresponsible and continue to cause us harm. It is honestly nerve racking being here at Jim and Anita's without you. Anita certainly wants me to feel like this is home a place where I can relax and be a part of their family during our three month transition, and although offered, they are not asking for grocery money. With that said...

I fully realize that you will not believe any of the following:

I took the time to really dig at myself during the drive over here and to figure out how best to reprogram myself over spending, credit cards, all the usual things that have been repeated cycles over the course of our marriage.......

I hope in my heart of hearts that we can grow closer in our marriage. I realize you have issues with me that you need to vent when we are stabilized down the road. I shall prepare for them. I am hoping to send this note as a Valentines card as I realize

you are the one for me

you are the heart of our house

you are very precious to me

I want to continue to take care of you for the rest of my life

We certainly have experienced and tested, tasted and endured, rejoiced and consoled each other over many things in 13 years of being together. We are not perfect individuals. I cannot hope to become the ideal husband or you the ideal wife. But we have a journey together and I feel we have kept God in our marriage but not as much as I should have. I want him re-centered there going forward even while we are apart.

There is nothing that will convince you except time and openness and prayer.

I will continue to pray for his guidance in everything we do.

Love, Matt

I answered him:

My Dearest Matt,

What a wonderful surprise to have your dear message. I logged on with the intent of sending you a Valentine. I love you sweetheart. I am so proud of you. You have had quite an endurance test over the past 4 1/2 years and you survived! That says a lot about you.

I miss you already. What an evening I had. Jeremy drew on the couch with crayons, Keith threw up for the first time and was fussy ALL evening long from the time he woke up from his afternoon nap until he went to bed. Plus, I had to help Eric with homework, try to get dinner on the table. Yikes! Single parenting is no fun!!!!

But that's not the only reason I miss you. I just miss having you around. I love you honey. Yes, I believe in you. I feel we have hit rock bottom financially which is perhaps what we both needed to change our ways. I have committed to giving faithfully and regularly to the church. Please hold me accountable to that. God has to come first!!!!! And I believe you have seen the light regarding finances and credit debt. So, here's to a brighter future!!!!!

And now we prepare for another transition in our lives with being apart for three months. Thank goodness for e-mail and phone calls.

Well, sweetie, our marriage certainly has endured a lot. I guess that's what commitment is all about. So much for my quiet time. Jeremy is at it again so I'll say good-bye for now.

I love you my precious Valentine,
Karen

Matt and I talked on the phone every day. Matt hated being apart from us and longed for the day when we could all be together. He kept saying how he didn't like this arrangement and he just wanted to come back to Michigan. I encouraged him to stay in Wisconsin because I felt he would have been even more miserable coming back to face unemployment once again. Uncle Jim noticed Matt's depression and had several talks with him. Uncle Jim helped Matt research Christian counseling in the area. Matt was open to this idea and was eager to get started.

On February 28, 2006, Matt celebrated his 37th birthday. He received a very special card from his parents along with this letter written by his dad:

Dear Matt,

It is 4:20 P.M. It has been a bright sunny day here at the condo. Mom had been running errands. I have been reading most of the day. Now it is time to put a few syllables on paper to help you celebrate your birthday. Are we to believe that this is number 37! Oh my, if we could tell you how much we have enjoyed your presence in our lives, you might not believe it all. But think Big,

Bigger, and Biggest....it would not even come close. Yes we have four wonderful daughters and their wonderful husbands! Then we have a wonderful daughter-in-law. As if these were not enough blessings for us...we have grandchildren and great grandchildren.

But we have only one son, an upright thinking, energetic, resourceful, caring and hardworking man of integrity who loves his family, his friends and works well with his fellow employees. He knows how to put in an honest day's work.

Matt, you love your wife, your children, and respect your parents. Your mother and I salute you, admire you, and love you. Happy Birthday and may God's richest blessings be with you and your family!
Love, Dad

Obviously the boys and I called to wish Matt a happy birthday. He sounded more down than ever before. I was at a loss for words at this point and thought Matt needed to hear words of hope from someone other than me. I suggested that he call our good friend Pastor Jonathan in Alaska. They talked for a while and Matt felt somewhat better.

Needing to desperately come home to see us, Matt asked his boss if he could take a few days off. "I can't explain why. I just need to be with my family right now."

His boss could tell something was wrong and replied, "Okay, take a long weekend and be back on Monday."

Matt arrived home in time to eat dinner with us. After dinner he told me he was going to the local hospital and wanted me to stay home with the boys. We kissed goodbye and I was full of hope because Matt was finally reaching out for help. I thanked God.

The doctor on duty gave Matt a low dose of depression medication and released him after talking to him for about thirty minutes. The next day we drove one hour to Traverse City and Matt's dad took Matt to a crisis center. Again, after talking for about thirty minutes, they sent Matt on his way. Matt's parents expressed their love, support, and encouragement to us. We all wanted to help Matt but didn't know what else to do. The fact that he was seeking help encouraged all of us. We thought the worst was over and that Matt would slowly begin to improve.

The following day we drove down to Macomb to spend the weekend with my parents. My mom watched the boys so Matt and I could go to lunch to celebrate his new job. Matt stared at his food the whole time and didn't feel like talking. He apologized to me for not being talkative. He told me to talk.

I told Matt how much I loved him and how proud I was of him. I told him I was looking forward to coming to Wisconsin next weekend to look at houses. Matt made a few nice comments regarding that. Then I made some silly comment about the boys and he snickered. I told him to reflect on all that God had gotten us through over the years. I assured him that we were going to be okay. We had brighter days ahead of us. Matt wasn't showing much emotion at this point so I paid the bill and we left.

We went back to my parents and my dad talked to Matt. A good friend of the family was also over and he was a trained Stephen's Minister. Matt seemed to perk up a bit and soon they were all playing ping pong and laughing. It was refreshing to hear Matt laugh.

The following day Matt reluctantly drove back to Wisconsin and went to work on Monday. Later that evening, Matt was on the phone with a Christian counselor for over an hour. He had an appointment scheduled with her for Tuesday evening.

Meanwhile, I was feeling very hopeful and encouraged that Matt's depression was finally out in the open and that he was receiving help. I desperately wanted to hear Matt's voice on Tuesday. I kept calling both his cell phone and work phone but he did not answer. I assumed he was in meetings all day and couldn't answer the phone.

CHAPTER 9

GOD OF HOPE

Tuesday, March 7, 2006 was a mild, sunny day. I was standing outside in the driveway waiting for Eric's bus to pull up and enjoying the beautiful weather. I noticed a car coming down the street that looked just like my parents' car. My first thought was that it couldn't be them. They lived four hours away so it would have been very odd for them to come unannounced. As the car got closer, I realized that it was my parents. "What are they doing here?"

They stepped out of the car and I looked at them and knew something was wrong. Something was very, very wrong. And then it hit me. I knew. I knew what they were about to say. "NO!" I screamed. "NO! Don't even say it."

They both ran to me and held me and said, "We are so sorry, Karen. Matt took his life this morning."

"No! No! No! No," was about all I could say. My dad took me into the house and my mom waited for Eric to come home. My dad was very calming and very comforting. I remember asking, "What do I say to the boys? I can't tell them."

My dad replied, "Don't worry about that right now. Let's wait until tomorrow to tell them. We need to make some phone calls. We need to call Matt's family."

"Call Mark and Kathleen first," I cried. Being concerned for Matt's parents, I asked, "What about Matt's parents? They can't receive the news over the phone. Someone has to be with them and tell them in person."

"Dad, call Pastor Jonathan. You have to call him. He has to preach at the funeral."

My dad was doubtful, "Karen, I don't think he will be able to come all the way from Alaska."

"Call him, Dad! If you don't, I will. I know this is what Matt would have wanted. Pastor Jonathan and Matt were friends. Please, Dad, please!"

Dad said sympathetically, "Okay, Karen."

I remember sitting on the couch listening to my dad as he made all the phone calls. I couldn't stop shaking. I just wanted Matt to hold me. I wanted Matt to comfort me. I just needed Matt so much right then. I couldn't comprehend the fact that Matt was gone. After a while my parents told me to gather some clothes and they helped pack suitcases for the boys. Our belongings were still in storage so we didn't have many clothes to pack. There was certainly nothing suitable to wear to a funeral.

My mom fixed dinner for everyone but I couldn't eat or even sit at the table. Sometime after dinner, my parents said it was time to drive downstate to their house. My mom drove my van. Jeremy and Keith were in the backseat sleeping. We had waited until their bedtime to make the four hour drive. My dad took Eric in his car. Mom and I listened to a worship CD for most of the car ride as I wasn't up for any type of conversation. My mom was telling me to start thinking of songs that I would want for the funeral. I did not want to make plans for a funeral. I just wanted to rewind time to when Matt was still alive. I had never seen my mom so shaken up. This was definitely a new side to her.

We pulled into my parents' driveway around midnight. I remember Chip and Sarah running out of the house to carry the boys inside. Chip and Sarah had been at a conference in Illinois when they heard the news. They had just arrived at my parents' house shortly before us. My sweet sister, Sarah, just held me on the couch. She was so comforting. Her touch and her silence meant more than any words she could have spoken. Eventually everyone went to bed. I could not sleep at all. I wanted desperately to fall asleep and wake up to find that this nightmare was over.

When I just couldn't lie in that big, empty bed any longer, I got up and started looking through pictures. Mixed in with all the pictures was the most comforting Bible verse. I read, "*May the God of hope fill you with all joy and peace as you trust in Him so that you will overflow with hope by the power of the Holy Spirit.*" Romans 15:13. I read it again and again and again. I clung to that hope.

And then I started writing. Memories of our life together were flooding my mind and I wanted to get them down on paper before they slipped away. I found comfort in writing this letter:

> My Dearest Matt,
> *I write this now so that our sons will know of the love that we shared. I remember our first kiss. We were sitting on Mark and Kathleen's couch watching a video and Brooke and Brad were spying on us.*
> *What an adventure we have had ever since. Our love was strong enough to endure a long-distance relationship from the beginning. You were always full of surprises. I will never forget you showing up in your dress blues in*

my dorm room the night the Persian Gulf War ended. Or the time you took me shopping for my engagement ring. And then our surprise marriage that shocked St. John congregation. And our fabulous renewal of vows a year later. Every time you wore your dress blues, I felt like Cinderella and you were my Prince Charming.

What a thrill it was to come visit you when you were stationed in Okinawa, Japan during your last year of you Marine Corps enlistment.

Your first civilian job after the marines – you were quality control manager at HMT and what a huge accomplishment for you to get them QS/9000 certified. You were also going to school part-time in the evenings to finish up your bachelor degree in Criminal Justice. You worked so hard and were always so ambitious. You really wanted a job with the FBI but I guess it just wasn't meant to be.

When we first started attending Living Word Church, we helped out with the youth ministry. Church was always an important part of our life. Later you became a trained Stephen's Minister.

And then our life took a surprising detour when your National Guard unit was sent to Germany. We were apart for seven and a half months. But hey, it gave you a chance to do full-time police work which was one of your many ambitions. And what an incredible week we had together touring Europe.

You were so supportive and encouraging with my decision to finish my bachelor's degree. Who would have thought that my A in Parenting and Family Skills would be immediately put to the test upon the arrival *of our precious Eric? Everyone told me how strong you were during Eric's heart surgery and the decisions you had to make. You spent your days at Children's Hospital holding Eric and then spent the evenings with me while I was in Crittenton Hospital. Oh, the joy and nervousness we felt bringing Eric home from the hospital with a feeding tube to deal with. You were such a happy, beaming with pride, new father. You were so good with Eric, and then with Jeremy, and Keith as well. You took them on so many special outings. You loved to take them hiking in the woods and I appreciated the countless hours you spent at the play lands so that I could have a few hours to myself. I smile as I remember all the wrestling matches you had in the living room with me shouting "Be careful".*

I want our boys to know what a hard worker you were and just so ambitious. You had a strong desire to constantly be learning and you earned a master's degree in computers. You enjoyed your job at Global Crossing so much.

Our years at Christ the King Church really helped our spiritual life to grow. We loved going to our small group Bible study and you usually led the opening prayer.

And then what an adventure we had in Alaska. Being a part of Zion Lutheran Church was definitely the highlight of our one year in Fairbanks. We enjoyed many Bible studies, family fellowship nights, our Monday lunch dates at church, the many close friendships, and the amazing worship experience at the contemporary service.

Many people have said that we endured more in our 13 years of marriage then most couples face in a lifetime. Yes, we had quite an adventure. After Eric was born, we dealt with his heart surgery. Our darling Jeremy was born a few months after 9/11 and also during your unemployment. And then lovable Keith was born up in Alaska.

Yes, we went through a lot but we also had so much love. Our love was strong enough to get through anything. But then the tragic day of March 7, 2006 occurred. It was the day that your heart stopped beating and the day my heart was broken into a million pieces. But rest assured, I may be broken but I'm not crushed. I will go through life being carried in the strong arms of Jesus. What a comfort that is to me right now! God is good. No, God is GREAT! God is always loving, always present, ALWAYS! I promise you, Matt, that I will do everything I can to make sure our boys know that Jesus is the only way to heaven. I will continue to do what you and I had started. I will provide them with as much spiritual nourishment as I can. There is nothing more important to me than Eric, Jeremy, Keith, and my salvation. I look forward to our reunion in heaven someday.

All My Love, Karen

I finished writing just as everyone was waking up. I couldn't sleep. I couldn't eat. I couldn't even function as a mom. I knew I had to say something to the boys, but what? How do you tell your sons that their dad is dead? My dad asked me if I wanted him to tell them but I said, "No. I need to do this."

"Boys, Mommy has something very, very, very sad to tell you. The reason we are at Grandpa and Grandma's house is because...............is because........'Help me God! This is so hard.' ....is because Daddy died yesterday."

Eric asked, "How did he die?"

"Oh Eric, Daddy was in his car when he died but it wasn't a car accident. That is all I can tell you right now. It is just so, so sad."

Eric said, "I don't understand."

"I know, Eric. I don't understand all this either." Eric (age 6) ran out of the room and Jeremy (age 4) just stood there not knowing what to think. I hugged him and told him how much I loved him. Keith was almost one so he had no clue what was going on.

The next few days were a blur. This week was supposed to be so different. I should have been making plans for Keith's first birthday but instead I was making plans for Matt's funeral. I do remember making phone calls asking Matt's friends to be pallbearers. I remember sitting in Pastor Mike's office going over the funeral service. I remember my dear friend, Patty, coming over to sit with me. Her understanding hugs were extra comforting to me because she had recently lost a brother to suicide. I remember my dear friend and former neighbor, Amy, coming over with appropriate clothes for Eric and Jeremy to wear to the funeral.

My dad took me to the funeral home to go over the plans for visitation. It was my first time seeing Matt's family since his death. We all just hugged and cried and said how much we love each other. The funeral director was impressed with how well we all got along. Everyone gave me the freedom to have the final say but I wanted everyone's input. I made someone else pick out the casket and the cemetery plot because I just couldn't do it. Matt's dad asked if Matt could be buried in his dress blues. I said no because they were in storage somewhere up north with all of our belongings.

My sister Sarah had helped the boys draw pictures and write notes to put in the casket so I brought those along. One of the boys drew a picture of daddy wrestling with them and wrote how much they loved wrestling together. Another sheet of paper talked about how much the boys loved daddy and how much they were going to miss him. Keith's picture had a big smiley face on it with the words: You were the best dad ever!

It was soon time for the visitation whether I was ready for it or not. I remember my brother driving Eric, Jeremy, and me to the funeral home. Keith was with my mom because he was too young to know what was going on. On the way there, one of the boys asked, "Is this the way to heaven?" And then as we pulled into the parking lot I remember hearing, "Are we in heaven?"

Peter chuckled and said, "No, it would be very disappointing if this was heaven." The boys couldn't understand the concept of seeing dad's body but knowing that he is in heaven.

The funeral director took Eric, Jeremy, and me into the room to view Matt's body. I cannot begin to describe the emotions that went through me. I wanted to stay close to Matt. I touched his arm but it didn't feel right. Eric kept his distance. He kept asking me to move away from daddy. Jeremy kept touching Matt's body and wanted to remain close by. I felt torn not being able to comfort my sons in the different ways they each needed at that moment. I felt relief when the other family members came in and yet I longed for more alone time with Matt's body.

There was a constant flow of people coming in the room. I sat on the couch because I was too weak to stand up. I couldn't believe how many people came. It was comforting and exhausting. I loved all the hugs. I felt stupid when people asked "Did you know Matt was depressed?" I retorted back with, "Obviously. But I didn't know he was suicidal." I loved hearing the stories of how Matt touched so many lives.

One of my favorite stories of Matt came from our good friends Gary and Denise. Gary had served in the National Guard with Matt. At the time of the funeral Gary was out of town receiving special training before heading over to Kuwait. Gary and Matt always thought that they would be serving in Kuwait together. Gary asked me for a picture of Matt so that he could take Matt with him. Then Gary said, "For as long as Matt and I have known each other Matt has been on my case about the importance of going to church on a regular basis. But more importantly knowing Jesus and having a personal relationship with Him. I know exactly where Matt is right now and if I ever want to see him again then I better make sure I know who Jesus is."

I was overcome with concern when I saw Aunt Anita and my adult cousins, Laura and Kim. They were the ones who found Matt and my heart just hurt for them. I wanted to keep hugging them. They were so strong for me. They were shocked with how good Matt looked and that we were able to have an open casket. Matt had shot himself in the head. I did not want any more details than that. They told me how sorry they were and how much they loved me.

Moments later I looked up and saw a face that brought immediate hope to me. There stood Gina who had recently lost her husband Matt to cancer. I did not know Gina very well but I had graduated from high school with her husband and I was offering my condolences to her and her two young boys just three months earlier. Seeing that Gina was surviving this ordeal and that she could come and offer me encouragement and hope meant more to me than words can say. What a strong woman she was! She was also real and honest. She told me how hard this was going to be but she also told me that I was going to get a chance to see just how strong God is. She gave me hope.

There was one more day of visitation and then it was Saturday, March 11 – Keith's 1st birthday. I couldn't have the funeral on Keith's birthday. I couldn't have a birthday celebration either so it was just a quiet day. I remember wanting to get out of the house by myself so I took a little walk. I cried out to God. *"What am I going to do? Where am I going to live? How am I going to raise three boys all by myself? How can I leave the boys to go to work full-time when they desperately need me now more than ever? I have no money. I have no job. I have no house. I have no church home. And now I have no husband. I am so alone. The friends I feel the closest to emotionally live in Alaska. This is too much for me, God. I can't do this. I am exhausted from the past few years of being under an incredible amount of stress and transition and now I have to go through this? How strong do you think I am, God? Because you are so wrong if you think I can handle this."*

I loved God's answer. These simple yet powerful words brought me immediate hope and peace. God told me, "Karen, my dear, you are going to be okay."

That's it. That is all He said. Oh, but there was power and tenderness in those words. The creator of the world just told me I was going to be okay. The One who loves me so much that He sent His Son Jesus to die on a cross for me, just told me I am going to be okay so how could I doubt that? I had no idea HOW I was going to be okay, but I knew I would be.

This was my moment of truth. I was facing the biggest 'mountain' of my life. In my human thinking, this was an impossible situation. There was no way I could 'climb this mountain.' My situation was too overwhelming – too despairing. I could not do it. Correction, I could not do it on my own. But my God of hope can do anything. This may be too hard for me but it is not too hard for God. As I cried, "Okay, God, show me what you're made of," my mountain of despair turned into my mountain of hope.

With a renewed heart I cried out, "I have nothing but my health, my children, and God and that is MORE than enough. God, You are truly all I need. I get it, God. I finally get it. As hard as this is going to be, I CAN live without Matt but I can't imagine living one day without You. I am so sorry that I once thought otherwise."

I went back in the house and told Pastor Jonathan what God just told me. Pastor had honored my request of coming all the way from Alaska. A member of the church paid for his plane ticket and I still don't know who that was. Pastor Jonathan handed me an envelope from our friends Eddie and Lori in Alaska. I opened it and started crying. It was a very generous check. They didn't want me to worry about finances right now so they wanted to make sure the boys and I had our immediate financial needs taken care of. I handed the check back and said, "I can't take this. I don't deserve this. I haven't been faithful in tithing and I don't deserve this blessing."

"Take the check, Karen, and here is another check from Sara and me. We love you and the boys. Let us help you in this way."

I can't quote him exactly but Pastor Jonathan said something about God's love, mercy, grace, and forgiveness and how no one deserves God's blessing. It is a gift given freely because of God's great love for us. Pastor Jonathan reminded me that we have a gracious and forgiving God. I was extremely grateful to God for His mercy and His love.

CHAPTER 10

OVERFLOWING WITH HOPE

The day of the funeral was upon us. I still hadn't slept at all. I was eating but only because my family was making me. For the past few days, I had not wanted to be dressed up. When you feel sick, you want to wear comfy clothes and that is how I felt. I thought I would start a new trend and show up to the funeral wearing sweats. I honestly thought about this. But then my attitude changed. I wanted to take a shower and I wanted to look my best for Matt. This was my goodbye to Matt and I wanted to be beautiful for him. When I was all ready to go, my dad looked at me and said, "You look beautiful, Karen." At that moment I wished those words had been coming from Matt.

My dad drove Eric, Jeremy, and me to church. He took us to a private room where we waited until the funeral began. Chip and Sarah waited with me. My cousin, Bethany, kept Keith entertained in the church nursery. Holding tight to Eric and Jeremy and with tears streaming down my face, I was ushered in behind the flag-covered coffin.

One of Matt's sisters, Ellen Marie, shared past memories of Matt and she also included the letter that Matt's dad had written to Matt on his birthday. She ended with, "I know that my brother, who loved his family so dearly, would never have taken his life if he was in the right frame of mind." We then sang "Beautiful Savior" at the request of Matt's parents. Pastor Mike prayed and read the scripture verses that we had chosen. We sang "Above All" and then Pastor Jonathan Goeke gave an amazing message of hope.

I recently watched the DVD of the funeral so that Pastor Jonathan's words would be fresh in my mind. Here is some of what he said. *"There is a cloud in the way. For some of you the cloud is guilt and I don't believe we can skip right over it. We need to dig in and figure it out. I'm sure you've said, "If only I had tried a little harder maybe something might have been different". Some of us are struggling with confusion. How in the world could it come to this? I don't get it. There is a cloud of grief over us. And I'll tell you the other one - anger. How could you? How could you?*

But the anger was diverted quickly. The anger was still there but it wasn't at Matt. The anger was at the thief. The one who comes to steal, kill, and destroy. Because this was a man of God and a man of faith and in a moment of weakness the thief used this thing called depression. I agree. He was not in his right mind. And in a moment of weakness the thief told him a lie and it looked like the answer. And so my anger is at the thief.

"Karen, I am amazed that you picked Romans 15:13. 'Now may the God of hope fill you with all joy and peace as you trust in Him so that you may overflow with hope by the power of the Holy Spirit." The cloud of anger, grief, and guilt makes it hard to see the hope but the hope is there because Christ is there. Our hope is not some childish wish. Our hope is found in the cross because in the cross we go and we find the forgiveness that we seek for Matt and for us. And in the empty tomb we find the key

to the fact that our hope isn't empty. We find Jesus Christ risen from the dead victorious.

I looked up a few of my favorite Psalms on hope. In Psalm 62 David says, 'Find rest, O my soul, in God alone; my hope comes from him. He alone is my rock and my salvation.' Psalm 130:7 says, "O Israel, put your hope in the Lord, for with the Lord is unfailing love and with him is full redemption." The last time I checked the word unfailing it meant it can't fail. I believe that the unfailing love of God covered Matt. I don't place my faith in Matt's faith. I place my faith in a gracious and compassionate God who sent his Son Jesus Christ who gives us hope.

1 Peter 1:3, 6 says, 'Praise be to the God and Father of our Lord Jesus Christ! In his great mercy he has given us new birth into a living hope through the resurrection of Jesus Christ from the dead…in this you greatly rejoice.' We don't greatly rejoice in each other's faith or in Matt's faith. We greatly rejoice in an awesome and powerful God. I fully believe in Matt's faith in Jesus Christ as the Son of God and the Savior of the world. We are not saved by our works. We are saved by the grace of God. In Psalm 145 we find the words 'The Lord is gracious and compassionate, slow to anger and abounding in love.' I cling to Christ and his death and resurrection because that is what gives us hope.

God is bigger than our humanity. He is bigger than our weaknesses and bigger than our struggles. And Karen, your God is big enough to take Matt - and your God is big enough to give you hope for today. 'May the God of hope (Karen) fill you with all joy and peace as you trust in Him so that you may overflow with hope by the power of the Holy Spirit'. (Romans 15:13).

I want to point to these words from "I Can Only Imagine." The second verse says, 'I can only imagine when that day comes and I find myself standing in the Son.' Matt had to change the words. God is the one who makes the judgment but it is my belief that Matt is in the presence of God. May God be with you as you celebrate the hope of

Jesus Christ in your life, in our lives, and in Matt's life. To God be the glory, Amen!

By the time Pastor was done preaching, I was overflowing with hope. As we were singing "I Can Only Imagine" by Mercy Me I wanted to stand up and put my hands in the air. I felt an incredible sense of peace, hope, and even joy. Pastor Mike was overcome with emotion near the end of reading my letter that I had written to Matt the morning after he died. I was emotionally strong enough to finish it for him but for whatever reason, I chose not to. The funeral ended with a video of pictures of Matt while the song "The Untitled Hymn" (Come to Jesus) by Chris Rice was playing.

I walked out of church with a lot more joy and hope than when I walked in. Unfortunately some of that joy was immediately taken away when I heard this comment from an unknown person. "I don't understand this. From what I just heard about you, you sounded like you were a good wife."

I heard, "Obviously you couldn't have been as great as everyone said you were because if you were then your husband wouldn't have killed himself." How I wished people would have hugged more and talked less. It was comforting to hear "I just don't know what to say." Or "I am so sorry for your loss." "Please let us help you in some way."

There was a bereavement luncheon at church after the funeral. In all the funerals my dad had ever attended, this was the most food he had ever seen. He was deeply touched by the outpouring of love from the members of his congregation. I wasn't focused on the food at that time but I was very grateful for all the volunteers who helped display the beautiful tables of food.

Due to the fact that the funeral was on a Sunday, we went to the cemetery on Monday. There were about 30 of us in attendance for the committal service. The boys and I were sitting next to Matt's parents. Everyone else was standing behind us and to the side of us. Pastor Jonathan said a prayer and read a few scripture verses.

Then the honor guard presented the flag to me with these words. 'On behalf of the President of the United States, the Commandant of the Marine Corps, and a grateful nation, please accept this flag as a symbol of our appreciation for your loved one's service to Country and Corps.'

I couldn't even cry. I just felt numb. I thought, *this scene is familiar from movies but this can't really be happening to me.* I didn't want a flag. I wanted my husband.

After the short committal service, most people left. A few of us stayed to watch the casket being lowered into the ground. I couldn't watch the dirt being dumped on top so we left. I spent the next few hours at Joanna's house with the Matzinger family. It was comforting being with them and sharing stories of Matt. We laughed. We cried. We promised to be there for each other in the days, weeks, months, and years to come.

The following days were a blur. My dad and I had to run an errand and I remember thinking, *Life is back to normal for the rest of the world. How can people be going about their day as if nothing has changed? I'm not ready for this. Where is the pause button? Everybody stop! I need to pause life for a while.* I lost ten pounds in ten days and went ten straight days and nights without sleep. My body was in a state of shock.

People from my parents' church were bringing over more food than we could possibly eat. In addition to the food, people were bringing bags of clothes, bikes, and scooters for the boys. A group of men from the church worked hard to finish my parents' basement. It was assumed that the boys and I would need to live there once Eric finished school in June. I was touched beyond words at the outpouring of love by people I didn't even know.

After spending two weeks at my mom and dad's, it was time to head back up north to Arcadia. My mom drove us and she stayed an extra day because my sister Sarah and her husband Chip had planned a birthday party for Keith. I was not up to celebrating Keith's first birthday. It was another reminder that life was going on without Matt. As I was helping Keith open his gifts, I felt like running out of the room crying and shouting. "How can we be having a birthday party? Matt just died. Doesn't anybody have a clue as to how I feel?" It was a huge relief when the party was over.

My mom had totally taken over caring for the boys and once she left, I was forced back into motherhood. What a blessing and a burden all at the same time. I had to get out of bed every morning and change diapers and care for my children. In taking Eric back to school, I was disappointed with the lack of concern from the teacher and school. The extent of their acknowledging our grief was an offer for Eric to see the school counselor. I didn't know the school families at all because we lived 20 minutes away and Eric was bussed to and from school and he had only been going there a few months. Eric was ready to be back in school and get back to his normal routine. He still hadn't realized the enormity of the loss yet.

Chip and Sarah were a wonderful support system for me along with the caring staff at Camp Arcadia. Chip was the director at Camp Arcadia which is a Lutheran Family Camp along the beautiful shores of Lake Michigan. The year round staff of five people brought meals and cleaned my apartment. Chip and Sarah invited the boys and me to eat dinner with them every night. I didn't want to burden them too much so after dinner the boys and I would head back upstairs to our apartment. The boys didn't seem to show many signs of grief during the first few months.

The boys and I headed to my parents' house for Easter weekend. How were we going to get through the first of many holidays without Matt? When I woke up Easter morning, I had barely enough strength or motivation to get out of bed. My mom was extra cheerful that morning and told me to look out the window. Immediately my tears of sorrow were turned into tears of joy. Scattered across the front yard were about 250 colorful, plastic Easter eggs. It reminded me of a rainbow and how faithful God is.

I opened up the front door to get a closer look and another surprise awaited me. Sitting on the front porch were Easter goodies for each of the boys. In addition there were two beautiful large Easter baskets for me with cards and gifts galore. I could not wait to show the boys. I suppose they reacted the way most young kids would. "This is the best Easter ever!"

The boys had a great time picking up all the eggs and opening them to find candy, stickers, or gum inside. I will always be grateful to my friend Patty and her church friends who secretly came Saturday night to bring Easter joy to our hurting hearts. In fact, this act of kindness touched me so deeply, that my friends and I now participate in this "egg ministry" as well.

We headed back up north the next day. Keith was a bit overdue for his one year check up. I had a few concerns regarding his development. He still was not crawling or saying any words. He played with the same toy all day long. The pediatrician noticed something unusual at the end of Keith's spinal cord. She told me to take Keith to the hospital for an MRI on his spine and brain. I started crying and said, "Do you have any idea what I have been through this month and now I have to worry about

Keith's spine and brain development? There can't be anything wrong with my Keith. I can't handle any more bad news right now."

I cried the whole way home from the doctor. I became very angry at Matt. "How could you leave me? This is so unfair. You get to be in heaven and I have to remain here on earth and learn to take care of the boys without your help. I am so jealous of you right now. I wish I was the one in heaven."

Venting my anger at Matt was not bringing me comfort. "Think, Karen, think!" "Pray, Karen, pray!" I cried out to God and put Keith in His Hands. By the time I arrived home and told Sarah the news, I was much calmer. Sarah, however, became unraveled and asked, "How strong does God think you are Karen? This is too much for you."

I think I ended up having to comfort her. Remembering the words my mother spoke to me seven years ago during Eric's heart surgery, I said, "God already knows the plans He has for Keith. I don't have to worry because God already knows."

Chip and Sarah were out of town on the day of the MRI. Matt's sister, Joanna, came to help out with Eric and Jeremy. I drove to the hospital in Traverse City. Matt's parents lived near the hospital and they came to offer support. They were a wonderful comfort to me. The MRI did not show any problems. "Thank you, God!" My pediatrician recommended I take Keith to a neurologist once I figured out where I would be living.

"Where will I live? What will I do?" With so many unanswered questions, I found great comfort in listening to praise and worship songs. There was a fantastic morning program on the local Christian radio station and the topic was the 23rd Psalm. I clung to every word and really got to know Jesus as my Shepherd and as my *everything*. The timing of the speaker discussing Psalm

23 was evidence of God's faithfulness! God is so great! I couldn't get enough of God.

I also found comfort in reading through the hundreds of sympathy cards that I received. It was overwhelming knowing how many people were lifting the boys and I up in prayer. I was aching to be back in Alaska with my Bible study friends. I needed them. I wanted hugs from them but I had to settle for phone calls. They sent care packages and pictures and notes of sympathy and encouragement. I appreciated every card and gift that I received but I especially loved the honesty of these words from my good friend Heather:

She wrote: How could I ever express the intense amount of sadness that I feel for you and your family? I do not know the answer. My heart is absolutely broken for you - I cannot imagine all that you have gone through. I can only hope that you are turning to God for the comfort you need right now. Only He can give you the amount of strength needed to bear such a tragedy. I pray for you, Eric, Jeremy, and Keith every single day – that you will find the strength and courage to make a new life for yourselves. Karen, I want to call you, but I am such a coward – I don't know if I could begin to find any of the right words. I know it isn't much Karen – but if there is ever any way I can help you – please tell me. I would feel so honored to help you with anything you might need, or even just want. Please give your sweet precious boys a hug and some extra love from me. I can't imagine what they must be going through. I pray and hope that you have lots of family help and support Karen. With so much love, Heather.

Her heartfelt honesty brought so much understanding. Before receiving this card, I couldn't understand why so many of my friends were keeping their distance at a time when I needed them so much. Now I realized that it wasn't that they didn't care. They just didn't know what to say or do.

Feeling overwhelmed and exhausted, I chose to mail out a typed letter to everyone instead of trying to write hundreds of individual thank you notes. In reading the thank you letter again, it leaves no doubt that God guided my every word because there was no way that I could have penned the following words on my own:

I am struggling with finding the right words to use to express my gratitude and appreciation for the many gifts we have received. Wow! I am overwhelmed by the outpouring of love. From the beautiful flowers, to the delicious meals, the babysitting, the gifts for Eric, Jeremy, and Keith, the generous gifts of money, the hugs, the phone calls, the cards, and of course the prayers - they all mean so much. I am filled with grief but also filled with hope. I loved Matt very much but I love Jesus even more. I know Matt loved me very much but Jesus loves me even more. And so, because of Jesus, I can find joy in each day. Because I am so weak, I feel God's incredible strength.......This may seem odd to some of you but here it goes. I have been blest beyond measure! God is so good and faithful. No matter what happens in life, nothing and no one can take God away from me. And He truly is all I need! Please continue to pray for the boys and me as life will not be easy. But...we are going to be okay and that's a promise straight from God to me!!!.............Overflowing with hope, Karen

The next day after writing this letter, I discovered that I would be receiving life insurance. I was shocked because I had assumed that life insurance was not available in cases of suicide. An incredible financial burden was lifted from me at that moment. God was yet again showing me His faithfulness. I offered up my thanks to God and also came humbly before Him and asked for wisdom and direction in what to do next. My first order of business was making sure that giving to God would occupy the number one spot on my new budget.

CHAPTER 11

A Lesson in Hope

I had no choice but to start a new life. After prayerful consideration, I bought a house in the same subdivision as my parents. We moved as soon as the school year ended. My dad mentioned the possibility of the boys going to the Lutheran school which was connected to his church. I was thrilled with this idea as I wanted the boys to get as much of Jesus as they could get. Eric was quickly enrolled in first grade and Jeremy in four year old preschool. I loved attending a Lutheran elementary school and so I was extremely hopeful that my children would have a wonderful experience as well.

Our household goods had been in storage since returning from Alaska. Moving day was packed full of emotions. What a blessing to be surrounded by friends and family willing to help unpack and willing to provide a shoulder to cry on. The boys thought it was better than Christmas when they saw all their toys.

With no man in the house I had to become somewhat handy and try to tackle putting the crib together. Thankfully my friend Jackie helped me figure it out. It was an exciting accomplishment knowing that I was capable of completing such a complicated task. It was also eye-opening that this was my life now. I was going to have to step out of my comfort zone and do the things that I used to rely on Matt to do.

What do I do with all of Matt's things? I wasn't ready to look through them yet, so I put the boxes in the basement. I thought about unpacking his clothes with the hope of him walking through the door but then I realized that wouldn't be a good idea. A friend recommended saving Matt's clothes and having quilts made for each of the boys. I liked that idea but I was not ready to cut up the clothes yet.

Moving week was long and tiring. It was exciting to be in a house after the many months of living with Chip and Sarah but it was also heartbreaking knowing that Matt would never walk through the doors of this house. How do we live in a house that will contain no memories of Matt? How do we let go enough and yet hang on enough?

As the final boxes were being unpacked, my friend Jackie invited me out to dinner. I was looking forward to a quiet, relaxing dinner. I arrived at the restaurant and discovered that several friends were there as a surprise birthday party for me. It took me a moment to catch my breath. I wasn't quite sure how to react. I wasn't ready for a party of any kind. My thought was, "Matt just died three months ago so why are you doing this?"

About half way through dinner I started enjoying myself somewhat. By the time we walked out to our cars, I realized what a blessing this night had been and I felt like I was given permission to be happy. My friends wanted to show me how much they loved me and that my life was worth celebrating. What a beautiful gift!

Was it really okay to feel happy? Was it okay that I wasn't crying all the time? Was it okay that I could look at my three sons and smile? Was it okay to leave the boys with my mom for a weekend and fly to Minnesota to see Megan who was one of my Alaska friends? Was it okay to feel angry at all my friends who were married? Was it okay to feel angry at Matt?

I was struggling with this new life. It was time for me to talk to a counselor. I felt guilty for feeling so angry at Matt. Countless times I would ask *"Why? Why would my husband choose to die? How could I not be aware of the depths of his depression? Why would my husband not open up to me about the emotional pain he was dealing with? Why am I left to deal with all the guilt, anger, and loneliness? Why didn't I stop him from going back to Wisconsin when I knew he didn't want to go back there?"*

It took many counseling sessions to work through the guilt. The breakthrough moment came when my counselor looked at me and said, "Karen, did you know that Matt was going to wake up that Tuesday morning and shoot himself instead of going to work? Karen, Matt had talked to several trained professionals within days of his death. Shortly after Matt's death you had a chance to talk to the emergency room doctor who was examining Matt. The doctor told you that he looked Matt in the eyes and asked, "Are you suicidal?" Matt said "No way! I have a wife and three kids at home. I would never do that to them." No one caught on that Matt was suicidal so why do you blame yourself for not catching it either. It's not your fault, Karen. It's not your fault."

She continued, "From everything you have shared with me, it sounds like Matt suffered from depression his entire adult life. Depression is far deeper than just sadness due to circumstances. Clinical depression is a mental illness. You cannot blame yourself.

You cannot blame others. You cannot blame Matt's unemployment. You cannot blame the military. You cannot blame any of your circumstances. Matt was ill. Matt lost hope. Matt lost the will to live. He wanted the pain to end. Matt chose to die."

The anger wasn't as easy to get over. There were times I would be pushing Keith in his baby swing and would picture Matt walking toward us. Instead of imagining running up to hug and kiss him, I would start yelling at him. "Get away from me! I don't want to see you anymore. You left me. You left your three sons fatherless. You abandoned us. How could you?" Obviously the anger was pretty intense at times.

When the grief and sadness became almost unbearable, I would fall back on the anger. It was easier to be angry than to be sad and lonely. Dinnertime and evening was definitely the hardest part of the day. It was tough being the only adult at the table. Not only that, but there was no motivation to cook a nice, healthy dinner. The boys were happy with macaroni and cheese, chicken tenders, hot dogs, and all the typical kid-friendly food. Keith was very sensitive to chunky food so I had to spoon feed him. My food was usually cold by the time I got to eat.

One day as I was crying to Sara (Pastor Jonathan's wife) about my meal time dilemma she shared a splendid idea with me. She got together with a neighbor friend one night a week when both of their husbands had to work late. She asked if I had someone I could do that with. At the time I did not so she prayed that I would meet someone willing to do that. A couple of months later, I met my friend Jenn and she loved the idea of eating dinner together one night a week. Jenn quickly became one of my best friends and one of my favorite cooks. Our kids enjoyed playing together as well.

Pastor Jonathan and Sara were a blessing to me in so many ways. I had many "address book" days where I would call everyone in my address book until someone answered the phone. Since most people have caller ID, I would wonder if people were avoiding me or if they truly weren't home. Pastor Jonathan and Sara always seemed to be the ones who would answer the phone. One of the things they did every time we talked was they prayed **with** me.

I would cry out to Sara about my parenting struggles. The boys not only had to learn to live without daddy, but were adjusting to a new town, new school, new church, new friends, etc. All those changes certainly had an impact on their behavior. Eric was seven at this time and he became a great helper. He LOVED vacuuming and would beg me to let him vacuum every day. It sounds wonderful that he wanted to help me but it also worried me. I didn't want him to feel like he had to become the man of the house. I wanted Eric to get to be a kid and enjoy his childhood. It also worried me that he wasn't showing many signs of grief. His grief came much later.

Keith was one and he adjusted the quickest to this new life. He was making some progress with his development but was still quite delayed. Twice a week he received physical therapy, occupational therapy, and speech. Keith and I both enjoyed going to his special school. Keith was clingy to me and I was carrying him everywhere we went because he still could not walk. It was physically exhausting.

Jeremy was now four and a half and his grief became very intense. How does a four year old grieve the loss of his daddy and the loss of life as he knew it? Jeremy's grief came out in anger. I was on the receiving end of that anger. My counselor told me to consider it a compliment because it meant that Jeremy felt secure in my love for him.

Jeremy would say extremely hurtful things to me. There were plenty of times where I vented to my friend Audrey. I would share with her the things Jeremy would say to me. Audrey was full of encouragement and great advice. "With every hurtful word Jeremy says come back with 'I love you.' You should notice an improvement over time." After a few months the hurtful words were replaced with 'I love you, Mom'.

Bedtime became a huge physical battle. Jeremy refused to lie down on his bed and I would have to hold him down. This would usually go on for one hour. He fought with his entire body. It was as if he was petrified to fall asleep.

Bedtime used to be a relaxing time of reading books, praying together, hugs and kisses, and night lights. Now it was the hardest hour of my day. I would leave Eric and Jeremy's bedroom in tears every night and cry out to God, "I can't do this anymore. Something has to change. I don't have the energy to go through this night after night. Jeremy needs help. I need help. How can I take Jeremy's pain away?"

I would hear God say, "You're right, Karen. You can't do this alone. But you and I together can. Remember, I am with you Karen."

One night God put it on my heart to call our pediatrician and tell her about Jeremy's behavior. I was hoping for sleeping pills for him or some other immediate fix. She recommended I take Jeremy to counseling. Within about two months of counseling, I started seeing drastic improvements in his bedtime behavior. We had finally reached a point where I felt comfortable leaving him with a babysitter. I was elated because that meant I was able to join my friend Kath's church bowling league. It was my only kid-free social outing and I looked forward to it every other Sunday. You could say that I was quite the enthusiastic bowler. I jumped up and down every time I got a strike. Obviously, I didn't get out of the house enough.

What an incredible blessing that I was able to be home with my children and not have to work full-time. However, that meant that I was with my children around the clock with no one coming home at the end of the day to relieve me. It was exhausting and very, very lonely. Realizing I needed a break, I asked my dear mother to watch the boys one morning a week so that I could attend a women's Bible study at church. One morning in Bible study I cried out that I was burnt out and could use some help. One lady responded and I was extremely grateful for her willingness to watch Jeremy and Keith for a couple hours a week.

Another answer to prayer came when my nephew Brad who was in his mid-twenties offered to come over on a regular basis to hang out with the boys. The boys loved wrestling with Brad and climbing all over him. Sometimes his girlfriend Laura would come to watch Keith so that I could scoot out of the house for an hour. Two of Matt's sisters lived within a 30 minute drive and they came as often as they could to lend a hand.

During conferences with Eric's first grade teacher, Mrs. Meyer, I started crying and shared how overwhelmed I was with all my responsibilities as a single mother. Finding quiet time to help Eric with homework was nearly impossible. Jeremy would get jealous and would act up. Keith was young and needed to be in the same room with me. I would usually have Keith on my lap while Eric and I attempted to do homework. Usually all four of us would be in tears within ten minutes.

Mrs. Meyer talked with her husband and he agreed to spend some one-on-one time with Eric. Our families had known each other for years. Eric was shy at first but he soon came to enjoy the attention he was getting from a Christian male role model. He also felt very special getting to hang out at his teacher's house.

Mr. Meyer was excited to help Eric with his pinewood derby car for cub scouts. Eric's car won for Best of Show.

Now that Jeremy's behavior had calmed down, Eric began showing signs of grief. Eric would get very sad and ask a lot of tough questions about Matt and about God. Eric found comfort in talking about Matt and looking at pictures. Eric loved talking about our time in Alaska. A highlight memory for Eric was going to the armory in Fairbanks and daddy showing him all the military vehicles. I don't think Matt realized that he was Eric's hero. Eric holds the military in such high regard and is filled with so much pride that his dad served in both the Marine Corps and the Army.

Eric began asking me how daddy died. At the time of Matt's death I told Eric that Daddy was in his car when he died but that it wasn't a car accident. "That is all I can tell you right now. It is just so, so sad." My counselor told me that if Eric continued to ask then I would need to tell him before he heard it from someone else.

The day before 'the talk' I had been told by the neurologist that Keith probably had a stroke as an infant and that is the reason for all his developmental delays. That night as I was tucking Eric and Jeremy in bed, Eric said, "Mom, we have to talk to Pastor Mike. I know Pastor Mike knows how daddy died so we have to ask him."

I told Eric that I knew. His face lit up and he said, "Oh mom, then tell me. Oh, please tell me!" Well, after the day I just had there was no way I could handle that conversation so I told Eric I would tell him after school the next day. I quickly sent out an e-mail asking for prayer coverage.

There was overwhelming evidence that we were covered in prayer. When Eric came home from school I was very much at peace. We started talking and the words came out straightforward and sincere. "Daddy died of an illness called depression. His thoughts and feelings were all mixed up. He didn't want to leave us. He just wanted the pain to stop. He loved us very much. He loved being your dad. He knew how much you loved him. He knew how much I loved him. He killed himself which is called suicide. Most people with depression take medication which helps them to not kill themselves. Daddy didn't get his medicine in time. He wanted help. He wanted to get better. It's just very, very sad. But boys, this is super important. God does not want anyone to kill themselves. God decides when it is time to die, not us."

Eric asked, "How did he kill himself?"

I answered, "Remember when I told you dad had died in his car but it wasn't a car accident? Dad was sitting in his car and he had a gun. He shot himself."

To which Eric responded, "I need to be a doctor when I grow up. Everyone in my first grade needs to be doctors. We need to build more hospitals so we can help people who are sick like daddy. We can't let anyone else kill themselves."

Wow! What beautiful, unselfish words coming from a seven year old who just lost his daddy. He wasn't angry. He was full of hope that he could help others.

CHAPTER 12

HOPE IS FADING, HOPE IS FOUND

As the holidays were approaching I began making plans to help the boys and I get through the first Thanksgiving and the first Christmas without Matt. We had Thanksgiving dinner at Kathleen's house with the Matzinger family. Despite all we had been through, we still had plenty of reasons to be thankful.

My prayer went something like this: "Thank you God for giving me such a trial that I have no choice but to rest in You. Thank you for tearing down my old soul and giving me a new one with deeper faith in You and a deeper love for You. Thank you, God, for allowing me to rest humbly at your feet. Thank you, God, for using my situation in a way that I can be a blessing to others. Thank you for giving me greater compassion to those in need. Thank you for allowing me to suffer so that my life can bring honor and glory to you. Thank you, God, for allowing my story to touch others, to heal others, to make others appreciate all that they have, and to allow each of us to appreciate all that you are."

My life wasn't all about Matt. My life isn't all about my children. My life IS all about Jesus. And so because of Jesus I can experience the true joy and peace that comes only from knowing Jesus, really knowing Jesus. In Philippians 4:12-13 Paul says, *"I know what it is to be in need, and I know what it is to have plenty, I have learned the secret of being content in any and every situation, whether well fed or hungry, whether living in plenty or in want. I can do everything through him who gives me strength."*

True contentment is found in those souls who have an intimate relationship with God. It is not about our circumstances. It is not about what we have or what we lack. It is not about our current mood. It is not a feeling. It is a way of life that is so deep down in the soul, that no one person or no one event, no matter how tragic it may be, can reach down and take it away. *"For I am convinced that neither death nor life, neither angels nor demons, neither the present nor the future, nor any powers, neither height nor depth, nor anything else in all creation, will be able to separate us from the love of God that is in Christ Jesus our Lord."* Romans 8:38-39.

My heart was desperately seeking more of God and in the process I was slowly surrendering my life fully to Jesus. However I had plenty of weak moments where I would fall back into self pity and self-centeredness. Those challenging moments came often during the month of December. It was then that I discovered that God truly is reliable, resourceful, dependable, sovereign, merciful, loving, and compassionate. God is good all the time. The character of God does not ever change even when our circumstances drastically change. How disappointing it would be to go through life thinking otherwise.

One of my favorite attributes of God is that of provider. The Father does so much more than just provide for our physical needs. God promises to grant rest for the weary. To those who mourn, God *"bestows on them a crown of beauty instead of ashes, the oil of gladness instead of mourning, and a garment of praise instead of a spirit of despair."* (Isaiah 61:3)

God gives wisdom to those who ask. God provides a way out when we are tempted. God offers forgiveness to those who repent. God supplies hope and second chances. God provides life and blessing as is very clearly stated in Deut. 30:19-20, *"I have set before you life and death, blessings and curses. Now choose life, so that you and your children may live and that you may love the Lord your God, listen to his voice, and hold fast to him. For the Lord is your life."*

A second attribute of the Father is that of refuge and strength. It is in those times of personal weakness that we get a taste of God's incredible strength and power. *"He alone is my rock and my salvation, he is my fortress, I will not be shaken. My salvation and my honor depend on God; He is my mighty rock, my refuge."* (Psalm 62:6-7)

Oh the peace that came over me during those moments of taking refuge in God. There were times of complete bliss but there were also times when I let the devil steal my joy and my peace. Satan would twist that peace and turn it into guilt. He would sneak up on me with these questions: "How can you possibly feel happy? What are others going to think about you if they see you so happy? What if they question your love for Matt? How can you begin to move on with your life? If you really loved Matt then why are you slowly letting go of him? What kind of wife were you?"

But Hallelujah! My God defeated the devil and so I stand in victory. I used the word of God to fight off Satan. My God promises that joy will come in the morning. *"I will turn their mourning into gladness; I will give them comfort and joy instead of sorrow."* (Jeremiah 31:13) *"Blessed are those who mourn, for they will be comforted."* (Matthew 5:4)

I wanted to bring comfort to the Matzinger family on Christmas Eve. The boys and I showed up at Joanna's house with a special gift. I knew that everyone was thinking about Matt. We all missed him, wishing he was still here. I wanted the family to talk about him. I came up with a good way to keep the memories alive and even share some laughs as well as tears.

Eric and Jeremy helped me write some of their favorite memories of Matt. We put them on separate slips of paper and put them in a gift bag. I passed the bag around the room and asked each family member to take one out of the bag and read it. Most everyone chose to add their own favorite memory of Matt as well. It was a huge hit and it helped take away the awkwardness of the "empty chair."

Here is some of what we wrote.

1. I had been working at a company for only two weeks when Matt had me arrested for the American Cancer Society. Real policemen came to my desk and handcuffed me and took me off to the pretend jail. I was so embarrassed but the next day at work everyone came up to talk to me.

2. Eric remembers Daddy teaching him to beware of dangers when they were hiking in the woods. Eric thought it was so cool that Daddy gave him a whistle to wear around his neck in case he ever got lost.

3. Often out of the blue Matt would say "Boys, put your coats on. We are going out." The boys always wanted to know where they were going but Matt would just say, "You'll find out when we get there."

4. It was a minus thirty degree day in Alaska and Matt was pumping gas. He was nearly frozen by the time he was done but he noticed a lady next to us pumping gas with no gloves, no hat, and her coat was unzipped. Matt

told her to get inside her car while he pumped the gas for her.

5. I remember that Matt had Veteran's Day off a few years back. He told me that he would stay home with the boys all day and that I could have the day off to do whatever I wanted. I remember getting my hair cut and telling the hair dresser what Matt had done. She had never heard of anyone doing that.

6. Matt would often start talking like Donald Duck and the boys and I would laugh so hard.

7. When we lived in Alaska Matt started the tradition of reading a Bible verse at dinner and then we all had the whole week to memorize it.

8. Almost every day Matt offered to give me a back rub or foot rub.

9. Eric remembers Dad making the coolest snow fort in our backyard.

10. Matt was a great teacher and very patient when he taught me how to drive a stick shift and how to use the computer.

11. Matt preferred to stay out of the kitchen as much as possible unless he was eating. I will never forget the time he was beaming with pride because he had set the table and said, "Honey, I cooked dinner for you tonight." Then he took a frozen pizza out of the oven.

12. Quote from Jeremy, "Oh I know everything! Daddy taught it to me."

Christmas morning was harder than I thought. It was just the three boys and I. Matt's absence was extremely obvious to me. The boys, on the other hand, were super excited with all their gifts. I went out of my way to make sure that they would have a good Christmas and it was fun watching them open presents. However, I spent over two hours putting together a castle that I had bought for Jeremy. What was I thinking? I must make a note to myself for next year not to buy anything that needs assembling. We spent the rest of the day at my mom and dad's house.

What helped me get through Christmas day was focusing on our trip to Alaska. Our very special Christmas gift was a trip to Alaska to see our friends. Eric, Jeremy, and I left on Dec. 26th. Keith was 21 months old at the time and still not walking. I thought it would be much easier to leave him home with Grandma and Grandpa, which I did.

It didn't bother me too much that it was 20 below zero when we stepped off the plane in Fairbanks. It was a week of non-stop visiting with friends. I loved every minute of it. Ever since Matt's death I needed to see my Bible study friends and get hugs from them. It brought so much comfort that I was able to do that. Knowing that New Year's Eve would be difficult I planned our flight home so that we would be on the airplane at midnight entering a different time zone. Midnight came and went without anyone acknowledging the New Year.

It was overwhelming facing the new year knowing that 2007 would not contain any new memories of Matt. For the last three months I had focused on going to Alaska but now that the trip was over I felt an incredible sense of loneliness and let down because of not having anything special to look forward to. And so the rollercoaster ride of grief continued.

I had spent many nights crying myself to sleep and feeling sorry for myself. During this time of loneliness I also discovered things about myself. I enjoyed reading Christian fiction. I enjoyed watching football on Sunday afternoons but it was nearly impossible to do so with the three boys needing my attention. I enjoyed socializing and having game nights. Unfortunately the boys and I didn't receive many invites. I didn't ask many people over because I too focused on how untidy the house looked. In reality the house was fine; it was my high expectations that were the problem.

Weekends were incredibly lonely. I was thankful for the Friday nights when Matt's sister, Kathleen, would come over. The boys and I also went to a small group Bible study every other Friday evening. Occasionally on Saturday evenings I would call my parents and ask if the boys and I could come over. Another person I could call to invite myself over was my friend Maryann. Maryann was widowed three months before me. She and I were at similar places in our grief and it was comforting to spend time with her. Maryann and I shared a strong faith in the Lord.

Another Godsend during this lonely season was my friend Brent. Three months after Matt died I was talking to the secretary at my former church in Fairbanks. She told me she was putting together bulletins for a double funeral. A young mom and her two year old had drowned in a tragic boating accident. My heart ached for the widower and his three surviving daughters. I immediately sent them a letter of hope and I received a beautiful thank you note back from Brent. He offered me his support and his friendship.

We quickly became friends and helped each other during this season of grief. A weekly phone call with the words, "Tell me about your day" was so simple yet so meaningful. Many times I shared my struggles of being a single mom and raising three boys. It was helpful having a male perspective. Other times I sent e-mails of hope and encouragement to him as he was a single dad raising three girls.

I loved God's provision and wisdom. He knew I needed a male friend but only a friend. I was not ready to date. The fact that Brent lived in Alaska and I lived in Michigan kept us at a safe distance and dating was never even an option. It was just an invaluable friendship with a handsome Alaskan firefighter.

God provided another special friend when He put Jessica in my life. Jessica had a beautiful heart to serve and to offer practical assistance to those who were hurting. A few days after I met Jessica, she was at my front door with a delicious meal. She was so easy to talk to that I openly shared my life story with her. She called me a few days later and offered to pray with me. We then began praying together every day. She lived two streets away and she would occasionally come over in the late evenings to watch a chick flick with me. Thank you God for girlfriends!

My first Valentine's Day wasn't as hard as I thought it would be. In fact it turned out to be a good day because I concentrated on my love for Jesus. I sent out the following e-mail on Feb. 14 with the subject "God's amazing love!" *I had just sent an e-mail to my sister-in-law in which I expressed glory and praise to God. As soon as I hit "send" I looked out my window and saw a neighbor (whom I had not yet met) plowing out my driveway. I used to think that "You can't out-give God" applied only to finances but now I realize it goes beyond that. I gave God praise and He immediately blessed me with a helpful neighbor. Isn't God amazing!!! I was filled with so much joy and peace.*

This Valentine's Day my focus is on God and His amazing love for us. When we stop to reflect on ALL that God has done for us how can we not rejoice? Being joyful has nothing to do with our circumstances. It has everything to do with knowing Jesus, really knowing Jesus as your Savior and as your Friend. And so today I am feeling the warmth embrace of Someone who loves me unconditionally. Someone who is always there for me. Someone who walks beside me whether I'm down in the valley or way up on a mountaintop. Someone who knows all my shortcomings and all my sins and loves me anyway. Someone who gives me renewed strength

*on days when I have nothing left to give. Someone who showers me with blessings and grace and mercy and forgiveness. Someone who has provided for me in ways I could never have imagined. Someone who promises to never leave me. Someone who loves me with an everlasting love.........
His name is Jesus! Happy Valentine's Day! Love, Karen*

And then Matt's birthday came exactly two weeks later which turned out to be much harder than I thought it would be. I got in my car to drive to Bible study but I just couldn't bring myself to go. I ended up at the cemetery instead. I sat there in my car crying not knowing how to spend the day. I wanted to eat a piece of cheesecake for Matt because that is what he always asked for on his birthday. Matt and I should have been celebrating today but instead here I was at the cemetery looking at his gravestone.

Knowing that March 7, 2007 would be a difficult day as well, I made plans to fly to Texas to see Pastor Jonathan and Sara and also my brother. Shortly after Matt's funeral Jonathan and Sara moved to the Houston area. My brother lived in Lubbock. It was a wonderful three days of relaxing, talking, and having fun. The change of scenery did me a world of good. Jonathan and Sara treated me like a royal guest. The time I spent with my brother and his girlfriend Jamie was wonderful as well. I enjoyed getting to know Jamie better and had strict orders from my family not to scare her away (said in humor). My entire family loved Jamie and we wanted Peter to marry her. On September 27, 2008 Peter and Jamie were married.

On the flight home back in 2007 I stared at my wedding ring and thought, "Why am I still wearing this? My ring is a painful reminder that Matt and I are no longer married." For fear of losing the ring on the plane, I waited until I was home before taking it off. My hand looked and felt empty. I was very much aware of the ring's absence and felt that everyone was staring at my hand. After a few weeks I panicked and put the ring back on. I didn't want to give the impression that I was ready to date because I wasn't. After a few months of taking it off and on, I reached a point where it stayed off permanently.

Shortly after returning from Texas I took the boys to the cemetery. This was their first time seeing the gravestone. Jeremy kept blowing kisses and Eric said that he hoped to have a new dad who would wrestle with him. Then he looked at me all worried and asked me if that would hurt Daddy's feelings because he said that. I assured Eric that dad would want us to be happy and that it was okay to hope for a new dad. I told him that my heart wasn't ready yet but that we could talk to God about it. Keith had just turned two and was full of smiles.

In April I attended a five week seminar for survivors of suicide. My friend Kelly had recently lost her husband to suicide so we went together. The seminar was extremely educational. I learned about the emotional pain that must have consumed Matt and how his vision must have narrowed to the point of only seeing the pain. He wasn't thinking about all the loved ones he would be leaving, he was only focused on leaving the pain.

I also remember the speaker talking about suicide as a tragic outcome of a serious illness. Suicide was not about moral weakness or irresponsibility. All the anger I had towards Matt subsided. In place of the anger was sadness. It broke my heart when I thought about the unbearable emotional pain that Matt had suffered. It was as if I started the grieving process over again but this time the sadness was more intense because the anger had diminished.

This emotional rollercoaster ride was exhausting and so I made the decision to go back to counseling. Here was another one of my honest e-mails dated May 2, 2007. *I have come a long way in a year's time but now my grief is different and pretty intense right now. It has been hard to live life at highway speed when you are still just learning to crawl. I don't think anyone can really understand that except for Gina, Brent, Maryann, and Kelly. And so I thank God for your love, friendship, support, and encouragement as we journey through our grief together.*

And I thank everyone else who have been there comforting me and helping out with the boys but it never seems to be enough. That isn't meant as an insult. I just need everyone to be aware that even one hundred people still can't replace what I had with Matt. I have had too many people lately tell me that they think I am doing great and I want to set the record straight. I am NOT great. I am still hurting and some days feel like I'm drowning. However, I am forced to continue on and be the best mom I can be for the sake of my three precious boys that I would do absolutely anything for. Please don't worry about me. Just pray for me as I have a lot on my plate right now. And PLEASE don't try to fix things. You can't. I have to go through the grief process and you all have to let me. So please back off with all the "helpful suggestions". But I will take all the hugs and prayers I can get. Thanks and hopefully I haven't scared you all away. Karen

My new counselor had his work cut out for him. This time I went to a Christian counseling center and it made all the difference. My counselor helped point out all the ways that God and others had helped me on my grief journey. God used many unexpected people and unexpected ways and I finally came to a point where I could truly appreciate all of them. My selfish and bitter attitude slowly was replaced with an understanding and forgiving attitude. It didn't happen overnight and I wish I could say that I never fell back into self pity or bitterness.

In late spring I was venting to my widower friend Brent. I was telling him how I needed people to help me out. My counselor warned me that I would go through the grief cycle a few times and how right he was. Longing to have friends and family surround me like they did back at the funeral visitation, I cried out to Brent. He immediately responded by sending out this e-mail to my friends and family.

My name is Brent and I live in Fairbanks, Alaska. Karen and I have become friends through life's unexpected challenges (the death of our spouses) and she has been an amazing part of my healing process. I have tried over the past year to be as strong as her and can't seem to keep it up. At my worst times, she always seems to come through, lift me up, hold me there, and let me know that I am loved and will be ok. I know we all have our bad times, and life seems to really get us down, that is why I am asking for your help. Karen sent me an e-mail this morning, and for the first time, she is asking for help. She states that she can't ask for help, but her e-mail to me is just that, a cry for help. If any of you live close enough, or have ties to her church, please try to lend some support to a very special friend of mine. I truly know exactly how she feels.

Within a matter of days, I sent out another e-mail. *"I just have to share this with all of you. Yes, I know about the email that Brent sent to all of you. Here is an awesome God story. I was sitting at my desk crying my eyes out (just having one of my moments) and literally telling God that all this is too hard. I hate feeling like this and I don't want to be alone anymore and I'm sick of asking for help because I don't want to be disappointed with a lack of response. Anyway, I was walking to get a Kleenex to wipe away my tears and I noticed a UPS truck in my driveway. I just received a huge cooler of delicious frozen meals from Omaha Steaks from my friend Karol who lives out of state. Wow! Not only is the timing unbelievable but the fact that God can connect a friend of mine in Alaska with a friend in New Jersey and together they can provide food to their friend in Michigan. And another Alaska friend is having one of her Michigan friends who lives just ten minutes away bring me over a meal on Sunday.*

With all this food I will be eating like a queen for weeks. Isn't it so true that we should never, ever underestimate the power of God!!!! I could share with you so many amazing stories of how God has provided for all my needs and all the dear wonderful people that He has used. So why is it that I still have so many bad moments? Thanks also to Matt's sister Joanna who is watching the boys today so I can have some peace and quiet. Doing the best I can, Karen

The bitterness was creeping back up. "Wait a minute," I thought. Brent must have sent that e-mail out to over 30 people and only about five people responded. And everyone seemed to have missed the whole point. I wanted local friends and family to invite me over for dinner. It was more about the socializing than it was about the food. "See God, this is why I don't ask for help. It is too disappointing."

But God so lovingly replied, "Karen, my dear, your solutions are different from my solutions. Would you have only been satisfied if all 30 people responded? You said yourself that even 100 people helping out can't replace what you had with Matt. Cry out to Me for help, Karen, and trust that I will provide the right people in the right timing. You can choose to be bitter to all those who didn't help you or you can choose to be grateful for the ones who did. Karen, choose to grow and learn from this."

Five weeks later I e-mailed my counselor: *"I just have to share this with you. I just had one of those life-changing God moments. I went to see <u>Evan Almighty</u>. God was totally talking to me the whole time. Then as I got into my car to drive home, the song 'The Voice of Truth' by Casting Crowns came on the radio. When the song ended the DJ said something about all you who are feeling lonely out there may you feel God's presence in such a powerful way. And then I looked up and saw the most beautiful rainbow in the sky. I starting crying to God, 'Yes Lord, I hear you. I recognize you. I am ready. I am ready for whatever you have in*

*store for me. I surrender. I surrender. I give you my life. I give everything
I have to you. I am willing! I.......Am........WILLING! Take me and
use me however you need to. I will obey. Take me.'*

"*Only a God like you can use me with all my flaws, doubts, insecurities,
fears, and sins and can empower me to change the world one random act of
kindness at a time. ARK – Act of Random Kindness (I got that from the
movie). I am ready and willing to go to the next spiritual level.*"

*You know that joy and peace and excitement that we talked about
today. I felt it. I really felt it. Wow! It was so powerful. I'm just so
energized and on fire right now. That tiredness and exhaustion that I felt
this morning, it is gone! Isn't God so amazing! His awesome timing!
I so needed to see that movie on the same day that I talked with you.
I am going to change the world with one act of random kindness at a
time! Thanks for all you do in helping me on my spiritual journey. You
definitely challenge me. God knew I needed a kick in the pants (or a boost)
up to the next level and He is using you to do it. God bless you and your
empowering ministry! Karen*

My counselor shared with me how moving up to the high
call of God will challenge every part of who I am. But there is
joy in being where God is calling me and joy in obedience. He
also warned me to watch out for the Enemy who will throw little
frustrations and discouragements at me to distract my climbing to
higher levels. But I love God's promise of protection in Ephesians
6:13-17. "*Therefore put on the full armor of God, so that when the day of
evil comes, you may be able to stand your ground, and after you have done
everything, to stand. Stand firm then, with the belt of truth buckled around
your waist, with the breastplate of righteousness in place, and with your feet
fitted with the readiness that comes from the gospel of peace. In addition
to all this, take up the shield of faith, with which you can extinguish all
the flaming arrows of the evil one. Take the helmet of salvation and the
sword of the Spirit, which is the word of God.*"

CHAPTER 13

HOPE FOR THE FUTURE

With spiritual growth came plenty of challenges and opportunities to serve. A friend in my ladies Bible study was suffering with leukemia. I heard some school moms talking about not knowing what to say or do. I quickly spoke up, "Well, we must do something to show we care."

God put it on my heart to offer the family practical assistance with bringing meals to them. I took a couple of meals over to their house but God showed me a bigger picture. I began a meal ministry at our church. I have to laugh that God should use me to start this. "Okay, God, I will do this but I really don't enjoy cooking nor am I a very good cook. I am a single mom with three young boys but you are asking me to do this so I know you will also equip me."

Before sending out the e-mail asking school families to provide a meal, I prayed that God would speak to all those reading it and that they wouldn't come up with excuses of why not to help. I was hoping for enough volunteers to provide the family with one month of meals. God yet again amazed me with His faithfulness.

There was such an overwhelming response that we were able to provide this family with four months worth of meals. In fact, right around Christmas time of 2007 the family approached me and said that the meals could stop.

It was during this time period that life began settling down. Was it because my focus was on helping others instead of on myself? Was it because I was more interested in pleasing God than in pleasing myself? Was it because I had finally handed the "pen" over to God to allow Him complete freedom to write the story of my life? I am grateful for all I have gone through because it has made me who I am today and I wouldn't want to change any of it.

It has been a hard journey and of course I still miss Matt. But I do not want my old life back because I do not want the old Karen back. My life may have been turned upside down, but my soul has been touched, restored, and renewed by the very heart of God. And so I can look to my future with hope, confidence and even excitement as I continue to feel God molding me into all that He created me to be.

In my brokenness I experienced the healing hand of God. I came to realize that I would not want to rob anyone of that same experience. As much as I'm sure my friends and family wanted to protect me and wanted to reach out to me, there was a part of the grief journey that I had to go through on my own. As I now reach out to others who are hurting I am careful to check with God before running to their aid. I'm sure we all have a list of times when we have let someone down by not helping out. Equally, there have also been times when we stepped in to shelter and protect and in doing so we interfered with God's plan.

I am grateful to all those that were part of God's plan in my healing process. Many of those people have already been mentioned throughout this book. There were countless people who prayed for the boys and me and we definitely felt those prayers. There were many practical things that people did to show their love and concern. My friend Audrey sent me several encouraging cards throughout the first year and also called me on a regular basis. My sister-in-law Ellen Marie called every week to check on me. She was usually full of hope and would tell me that life would get a bit easier as the boys grew and could do more things for themselves. Matt's parents called often to check on the boys and me. My life-long friend Jill called consistently.

Norine befriended me at Bible study when I was new to the church and school and desperately needed a friend. Being a single mom herself, she was able to encourage me and offer words of hope from an understanding point of view. My younger cousin Bethany took time out of her busy college schedule to spend a weekend with the boys so I could have two days to myself. I used that time as a personal retreat with God. No phone calls were made and all I brought with me were my Bible and my scrapbooking bag. I came home feeling refreshed and ready to begin a new year.

We have a God who specializes in doing the impossible. God took my broken heart that was shattered into a million pieces and built a bigger, stronger heart. A heart big enough to trust and accept love again. Even before I felt ready to open up my heart to begin dating and risk rejection I told God all the qualities I would want in a future husband.

I did not ask for fame or fortune or all those things that the world deems important. I wanted a man who had Godly characteristics. I wanted someone who truly loved God above all else and would understand that I would love God more than I loved him. I wanted someone who was joyful and could appreciate the work of God as it was happening. I wanted someone who would love me and accept me for who I am in Christ and someone who would both challenge and encourage me to continue growing closer in my relationship with Christ. I wanted someone who would pour love into the lives of Eric, Jeremy, and Keith and take them as his very own children. I wanted someone who had never been married before and who was saving himself for his future wife. My list went on and on and I asked a lot of God.

At first I allowed myself to believe that my list was too much and that I was asking the impossible. I thought, "Surely a man like that doesn't exist and if by slight chance he does, he certainly wouldn't still be single." But quickly that attitude changed into this, "I have a God who parted the Red Sea. Surely He can create a man like this, keep him single all these years, and bring him into my life at just the right time."

But it didn't stop there. I then gave up complete control of this issue and gave it all to God. The boys and I prayed this prayer together every night. "God, since you are so much smarter and wiser than we are – we trust You. When You feel we are ready, please bring the right man into our lives. Someone who not only loves Mom but someone who will love us as well. But most importantly God, someone who loves You above all. Amen."

I had reached a point where I felt ready to date but I didn't feel comfortable joining an on-line dating service or even attending any single groups at local churches. I did not feel comfortable telling many people including my own family. I confided in a few close friends and they began praying.

One fear I had about dating was that I didn't want to lose the passion I had for Jesus. Jesus had truly become the lover of my soul. I did not want a man to come between Jesus and me. I knew that God would have to bring a man into my life who was just as passionate if not more passionate for Jesus than I was.

Back in August of 2007 the boys and I had been vacationing at Camp Arcadia, our favorite vacation spot. Many of the campers and cottagers were aware of my story and I could feel the love of the entire camp community. One of the ladies I met told me that she had been praying for the boys and me for the past year and a half. It was humbling to know that someone we had never met had been covering us in prayer.

After talking to me throughout the week she mentioned to me that she had a cousin who she thought I might be interested in meeting. When she told me that he lived out of state, I told her I was not interested at all in a long-distance relationship. I believe God used this wonderful lady to confirm the fact that I was ready to date. I know I didn't need permission but I have to admit it was nice to have it.

During the fall of 2007 when I was putting my energy into organizing the meals for my friend with leukemia was when God used a mutual friend to introduce me to a man named Lee. Lee was truly everything on my list and more. We e-mailed and talked on the phone for about five weeks before meeting in person. By the time we had our first date, Lee and I were already friends and I didn't feel too nervous. He said the most beautiful, heartfelt prayer on our date which I found to be incredibly romantic.

It had been nearly 20 years since I had gone on a first date so I was a bit rusty. Looking back I can laugh at some of the things I said as it was definitely not your typical, light-hearted first date conversation. I think I violated almost all the things of what not to say on the first date. In other words, I talked mostly about Matt. Apparently I didn't scare Lee away because nine days later we had our second date at his work Christmas party.

My friend Norine said, "Wow, Karen! He must really like you if he's taking you to meet all his co-workers."

Lee was a gentleman and honored my request of no kissing for a while. I needed this relationship to move very slowly but I also knew that Lee had to set the pace, not me. The great thing was that Lee let God set the pace. We were both very real with each other and became very good friends.

After four months had gone by, we both felt it was time for him to meet the boys. We prayed about how to go about it. Eric's counselor recommended we have a game night at a friend's house where the boys felt comfortable. I asked my friend, Maryann, if she would be willing to host the party. She and her newly married husband, Ken, were glad to do it and extremely supportive of my new relationship with Lee.

Maryann Gilliam was no stranger to heartache and tragedy. On Christmas Eve 2005 her husband, David, died suddenly in their home and left her to raise their six children ranging in age from twelve to three weeks old. Maryann was advised to vacate her home due to dangerous levels of toxic spores in the basement, which may have contributed to David's death. She and her children moved in with family and friends and eventually were blessed with a beautiful home built by ABC's hit show: Extreme Makeover: Home Edition. God used this home to bless our family as well as this would be the location where the boys would meet their future stepdad.

I was not to introduce Lee as my boyfriend. Lee was just a guy who was at the party. It was a very small party with just a few good friends, my parents, and my sister, Jennifer. Everyone knew the plan. After dinner I would ask, "Who wants to play Uno Attack?" The boys loved that game so I knew that they would say yes. Lee said he would play and everyone else knew that they were not allowed to play.

Playing the game with the boys was a great way for them all to interact without feeling awkward. The boys had a lot of fun with Lee. It was neat to see them joke with him. My friends and family noticed how great Lee was with the boys and with all the kids at the party. They were all so happy for me and very supportive of our relationship.

Next came a phone call that I was extremely nervous to make. I knew I needed to call Matt's parents and tell them I was dating before they heard it from someone else. The reaction from Matt's mom was priceless. She said with all sincerity, "I am so happy for you. This is the best news I have heard in a very long time. You need someone in your life and so do the boys." She told me that she would pray for Lee. She then asked me to tell her all about Lee.

"Lee is a spirit-filled man who lives to serve God. He is 44 years old and has never been married. He has always wanted a wife and children but has been waiting for God to bring him the right one. Lee lives in Port Huron which is 45 minutes away from my house. He works at a funeral home. He is kind and gentle and funny. He loves spending time with his nieces. Lee volunteers at his church and also in the community as assistant scout master with the Boy Scouts. The boys really like him but they don't know we are dating yet."

Up to this point, Lee and I had not gone out on a date in my town. He wanted to take me out to a restaurant in close proximity to my house. I was extremely nervous when we walked into the restaurant and thought, *What if someone I know sees me on a date? Will they be happy for me? Will they think this is too soon for me to date? How do I introduce Lee?*

We made it through dinner without running into anyone that I knew. The next day I called my widow friend Gina and told her about my date and how I felt like I was cheating on Matt. She chuckled, "Karen, you definitely were not cheating on Matt. Your marriage ended the day he died. It is okay for you to date. You don't need anyone's approval but God's. People will have their opinions and some will voice them to you. Your main concern will come when the boys learn of your relationship with Lee. Take it slow for the sake of the boys. They have to be on board with this in order for it to be successful."

Having Lee in my life did not mean I was no longer missing Matt. Lee was understanding of my need to talk about Matt. There were times I cried and told Lee how much I missed Matt. Lee would ask me if I wanted to talk about how I was feeling or if I wanted to be alone. "Karen, you and Matt were married for 13 years. You had three kids together. I would worry about you if you didn't talk about Matt."

March 7, 2008 was approaching. This marked the two year anniversary of Matt's death. I spent time praying about what to do on that day. God put it on my heart to do something special for someone. Since the military had been such a big part of our life, Eric, Jeremy, Keith and I made cookies and brownies to take to the local Air Force Base. I used to affectionately call Matt my cookie monster. I had called a member of our church who worked on the base.

Lieutenant Colonel Robert S. Nicholson agreed to bring the boys and me on base and show us around. The boys and I were able to sit in some of the planes and also talk to the airmen. I remember Eric's comment that day. "This is one of the most exciting days of my life!" It was a rough day for me as it brought back so many memories of Matt in uniform. I kept expecting him to walk through the door.

After seeing Lee and I interact on several occasions, Eric figured out that we were dating. Eric wasn't too sure about this. "No one should be kissing you but dad."

Jeremy said, "If you love each other does that mean you are going to get married?"

Keith was too young to remember his dad so he was very receptive to Lee and just clung to him.

After they got to know Lee better, I asked the boys if they felt Lee was the answer to our prayer. They all said, "Yes!"

I happily thought, *Good. This is very, very good. Now we just need to sit back and wait for God to tell Lee that we are the answer to his prayers as well.*

Lee spent many Saturdays at our house. It was obvious that Lee had not only fallen in love with me but with the boys as well. The boys enjoyed wrestling with Lee, doing yard work, going on fun outings, watching cartoons, and just hanging out. As the months went by I thought it would be a good idea to give Lee and the boys an opportunity to spend a day together without me. I went off to a women's retreat for the day.

When I arrived back home I was greeted with the smell of homemade chocolate chip cookies. Lee told me how the boys helped him mix the ingredients for the cookie dough. He laughed as he shared with me Jeremy's comment, "This isn't the way my mom makes cookies. She opens a package and places the dough on the cookie sheet."

I joined Lee in laughing and said, "This is why God blessed me with a man who enjoys cooking and baking."

On the one year anniversary of our first date, Lee took me back to the same restaurant so we could relive our first date. He said the most beautiful prayer thanking God for our relationship. After our plates were cleared away, he handed me a card. He wrote: "*Karen, I just wanted to say how much I love you. You are an answer to prayer. Thank you for striving for God and putting Him first. The last 12 months have been the most remarkable and enjoyable times in my life. Thank you for being part of God's plan and letting Him bless me with getting to know you and the boys. I am truly blessed to have you as a part of my life and am looking forward to what God has in store for us as we continue our walk together with Him at the forefront*".

"*Thank you Lord for this wonderful woman you have allowed me to come close to. Thank you for her spirit, her heart and her love for you. Thank you for the blessing she has been to me. Continue to shower your love on her and to see how much you love her. Thank you for her love and let her know and see how much she means to me. Amen. I love you, Karen.*"

With tears in my eyes I looked up at Lee and he came over to me, got down on one knee and asked me to marry him. I was completely stunned. I am very hard to surprise but Lee managed to pull it off. I think I gave him a blank stare for about a minute and then finally said "YES! I would be honored to be your wife."

Before we said goodnight we prayed and asked God to help the boys accept this news. We knew that Keith and Jeremy would be thrilled but we were wondering how Eric would react. I love God's perfect timing. We were engaged on a Sunday night and there ended up being no school that Monday because of a snow day. It worked out great having the boys home with me all day so that I could observe them and get a feel for their true reaction. Another benefit was that Eric had a counseling session scheduled that Monday afternoon.

As soon as all three boys were awake I told them that Lee and I were getting married. The e-mail I sent out the next day captures it all. "*Eric jumped up and down, clapped, was beaming from ear to ear, and shouted, "YES! We get to have a daddy again. I want Lee here with us every day.*" The boys are as happy as I am. This all truly *is a HUGE, incredible answer to prayer! Celebrating in the Matzinger home! Karen*

I sent the following e-mail to Jeremy's first grade teacher: "*Lee and I are engaged. Keep your ears open to hear if Jeremy says anything about it. He has been wanting Lee and I to get married for the past several months and now that we are, he had a surprising reaction. He tells me he doesn't want to talk about it for three days. I think he is hiding his excitement for some reason.*"

When the three days were up I asked Jeremy how he felt about Lee and I getting married. Jeremy told me how excited he was and that he knew that Lee was going to be a great dad. I still couldn't figure out why he had the three day waiting period before he expressed his enthusiasm. Later that week Lee came over and took us to Chuck E. Cheese to celebrate the fact that we would soon become a family.

Three weeks had gone by since the engagement and I found myself sending another emotional e-mail to a friend. "*Lee and I were talking last night and we wanted to share this with you. Lee and I both seem to have this cloud of heaviness over us. It pains me to see Lee hurting and feeling overwhelmed with work issues and also all the changes he is facing with marrying me. I want to fix it but I know I can't. Lee's insecurities bring out my insecurities. Is Lee really ready for this? Am I really worth it? Will I really be that good of a wife? The last person that married me ended up killing himself. I don't want that to happen to Lee. I know, I know, I know that Matt's death was about his depression and not about me as a wife. And then this whole wedding planning has caused a lot of the grief to resurface. This is just another confirmation that Matt really is gone and not coming back.*

I love Lee so very much and I am honored to be asked to be his wife and I look forward to it. I know this is what God wants. I have never been more sure of anything. So, this feeling of heaviness and grief just really took me by surprise."

Over the course of the next few weeks Lee shared more of his insecurities with me. He was ready to marry me but he knew he would be making a lot of changes and that scared him. He had lived in Port Huron his entire life so the anticipation of him moving 45 minutes away was a big deal to him. Lee agreed with me that it was important for the boys to remain in their house and in their school. They had gone through enough moves and changes in the last four years.

Lee was also going from bachelorhood to married with three children. This was something he had prayed for but he was feeling an enormous amount of responsibility and insecurity. He was wondering if he would be a good provider. Would he be a good spiritual leader in the home? Would he be able to handle his role as head of the house? These questions were weighing heavily on his mind. We spent a lot of time in prayer. Lee and I knew that our relationship was from God and that God would bless our marriage. We went to pre-marriage counseling and used the workbook Before You Say "I Do" by H. Norman Wright and Wes Roberts. This workbook was extremely helpful and provided hours of deep, meaningful conversation regarding our expectations of marriage.

Although this was my second wedding, it was Lee's first and he wanted a traditional wedding complete with groomsmen and bridesmaids. We prayed over the guest list and the songs and every other detail we could think of. We wanted to make sure that the focus was on God and not on us. God was the one who was writing our love story. God was the one who was at work through all of the events leading up to this day. God was the one who had been faithful. God was the one who had given us hope. God was the one who had a purpose and a plan even in the most difficult and challenging of circumstances. God was the one who had been preparing us to reach this point in time where we would be joined together as one.

We were grateful that all the wedding plans were falling into place including this wonderful surprise. Beth Merritt, of Beth Merritt Photography, was so touched by our story that she contacted us and asked if she could have the privilege of photographing our wedding. She had chosen to stop working at weddings and was enjoying her more relaxed settings for quite some time but was willing to make an exception in our case. The blessing that left us speechless was the fact that she offered to do it free of charge.

When the big day arrived, I was not nervous at all. Nothing I had ever done in my entire life felt as right or as blessed by God as this most memorable day. On July 26, 2009 Eric, Jeremy, and Keith walked me down the aisle and the five of us became a family. It was the same aisle we had walked down three and a half years earlier in horrible disbelief as we followed a coffin. Now here we were under very different circumstances with smiles a mile wide. My black dress of mourning had been turned into a beautiful yet simple white wedding gown. Oh the redemptive love of God!

As we walked down the aisle, a million thoughts were running through my mind. "Thank you God! Thank you! Thank you for the healing that has taken place not only in my life but in the boys' lives. Just look at them. Eric, my 10 year old, looks so grown up and more like Matt every day. Thank you that he has been off all his heart medication for years and that he only needs annual heart check-ups. He continues to have a tender, compassionate, serving heart. I am so proud of him. The nurse in the hospital was right when she told me that Eric would be an incredible blessing to our family."

And what a complete transformation I have seen in Jeremy. My seven year old is an absolute joy to be around. "Thank you, God, that his aggression toward me has been changed into gentleness and loving affection. Thank you for the athletic and academic talents you have given him along with his fun sense of humor."

And then I am in awe as I look at Keith who is now four years old. Oh how I prayed and prayed that he would walk and talk and now I have to tell Keith to sit still and be quiet. If I were to let go of his hand right now, I know he would run down the aisle and jump into Lee's arms. "Thank you, God, for the contagious joy and happiness that you placed inside Keith and oh how he loves you Lord."

And then look at Lee, my handsome groom, waiting for us so patiently and so full of love. Lee is everything I had prayed for and so much more. "I love him Lord, but help me to never love him more than I love you. I love you Lord. Thank you. Thank you for this day. Thank you for the promise you spoke to me three and a half years ago when you told me I was going to be okay. I am more than okay. Thank you God!"

How appropriate that the bridesmaids had just walked down the aisle while the hymn *Give Thanks* was playing. The words to the hymn said it all. 'Give thanks with a grateful heart. Give thanks to the Holy One. Give thanks because He's given Jesus Christ, His Son. And now let the weak say I am strong. Let the poor say I am rich because of what the Lord has done.'

CHAPTER 14

A BREATHTAKING VIEW OF HOPE

We recently celebrated our one year anniversary. I had originally planned for just the two of us to go out for dinner. However, earlier in July Eric asked, "Mom, what are WE going to do to celebrate the day we became a family?" Our romantic dinner plans were quickly changed into a kid-friendly restaurant with a table for five.

What an incredible answer to prayer that the boys have lovingly embraced their new dad. Keith began calling Lee "Dad" from the day of the wedding. Eric and Jeremy took much longer which was very understandable. They needed to reach a point where they could say, "We wish our first dad was still alive to raise us but he's not so we are glad that God brought you into our life. We love you, Dad." I love God's timing in that the switch from 'Lee' to 'Dad' occurred just weeks before this book was printed.

With all that I have been through I realize that we all face mountains during our journey here on earth. Some of us seem to run into mountain after mountain. Perhaps you are facing a mountain right now and are in desperate need of hope. Is your marriage crumbling? Do you suffer from depression? Are you unemployed? Are you in a financial crisis? Are you battling an illness? Are you lonely? Are you a single parent? Are you feeling overwhelmed? Are you dealing with some type of abuse or addiction? Are you in the middle of a life-changing decision? Are you dealing with the death of a loved one?

Whatever the mountain, there is hope. Because we have God we are never, ever without hope. Isn't that comforting? God CAN and DOES move mountains. What can be difficult to accept and understand is that it is not necessarily in our timing and in our way but God is always faithful about keeping His promises.

There are hundreds of promises in the Bible. Cling to those promises. My favorite promise from God is found in Joshua 1:5b, *'I will never leave you nor forsake you.'* How comforting to know that no matter what happens to me, God will never abandon me. Our God is a God of love and compassion.

My dear friend Audrey wrote a poem titled: "Pressing On." As an introduction to her poem, she wrote: *"I have often heard people use the metaphor of having to climb another mountain in their life, referring to the challenges they are currently facing. Well, hiking down and up the Grand Canyon for two days gave me a lot of time to think about this metaphor. God gave me an awesome visual aide that helped me put some issues into perspective. So, I felt inspired to write this poem on my Grand Canyon experience.*

There were several trails that you could choose to go on at the Grand Canyon, some were paved and others were in varying degrees of ruggedness. Everyone has picked their own trail in life. Ted and I chose to challenge ourselves by picking one of the more rugged trails. While hiking on the trail I learned that it is important to keep my focus and always know where I am going to take my next step. When I was not paying attention I would lose my footing and slip. No matter how rugged my trail is in life it is important to always keep my focus on God.

We often came across droppings left by the donkeys. On some parts of the trail it was more like an obstacle course to avoid stepping in the droppings. Sometimes you had no choice but to step in it and just deal with it. I have come across a lot of obstacles in my life, some too big to avoid and I wonder 'how am I going to press on?' God is testing me and I have learned that how I handle each of my obstacles will reflect and impact my life in some way.

Ted and I would often stop and rest along the trail and revive our bodies with water and food. My body was tired and my muscles ached. But when we took the focus off of ourselves and looked up we saw God's beautiful masterpiece right in front of our eyes. No words or pictures could describe how beautiful the Grand Canyon really is.

In my life I found it is important to feed my soul some spiritual food every day, to humble myself before God and thank Him for all that He has done for me. After our rest time we would frequently say, "It is time to press on." Our trail usually went back and forth across the mountain which is called a switchback. I didn't feel like we were making much progress this way, but when we came to a clearing, we could look down and see how far we came.

In my life I have taken a lot of turns and some were not good choices. In the midst of it all I wonder if I really made any progress in my life. I can get discouraged and I become impatient with my slow progress of changing my ways, but step by step God has been faithful in guiding me along my journey.

We encountered all kinds of weather. We had hot (average 110 degrees), rain, lightning, thunder, and strong cool winds. I had to constantly remind myself that God was in control of it all and I asked Him to just give us only what we needed. That is when it started to rain which felt refreshing because we ran out of water and had been walking for several hours without it. The rain was exactly what we needed.

God kept me focused when I was tired and weary. Bible verses that I had memorized in the past came to my mind and I repeated them to myself constantly. He reminded me of His faithfulness in the past and His promises. Night came before we made it to the top. We turned on our flashlight and as long as I focused on the light I was not afraid. I thought about the times in my life that I was lost and walking in darkness. I had been given the right tool (the Bible) but I didn't know how to apply it to my life. The flashlight would be useless unless I knew how to turn it on. My journey with God has had its challenges, but if I can put my hope in Him, remember His faithfulness and promises, I will be able to get up and "press on toward the goal..." Philippians 3:4

PRESSING ON by Audrey Maag

I am on a long journey,
I have a big mountain to climb.
Lord, what should I be learning?
There are obstacles that I must face.
Help me to deal with these challenges,
So that I can encourage others in the race.
How will I keep pressing on?
When at times I feel like giving up,
Everything seems to go wrong.
I know I carry a lot of stuff.
It causes me to stray from You.
How can Your word really be enough?
I need to stop and rest,
For I am tired and weary.
How will I pass this test?
I have taken many turns in my trail,
I wonder if I have made any progress.
Please give me patience, so I will not fail.
All kinds of weather have come my way.

Lord, I know You are in control of it all.
Please encourage me throughout my day.
Help me to focus on Your guiding light.
And allow You to lead me out of darkness,
So I can learn and do what is right.
I need to put all my HOPE in You.
Help me to remember Your faithfulness,
And Your promises to help carry me through.

Audrey concluded with Hebrews 10:23. *"Let us hold unswervingly to the hope we profess, for he who promised is faithful."*

I am enjoying living my life letting God be in control and not holding on too tight to anything or anyone but realizing that everything I have is a precious gift from God. I have experienced many extremes in life and I know that life is much easier when you stay focused on Jesus instead of on yourself and your circumstances. Perhaps our prayer shouldn't be to ask God to move our mountain but to ask God to help us see the mystery and the strength of the mountain. And then, when He is ready to move the mountain, stand by and prepare to be amazed.

Hope does not mean you are confident that everything will work out the way you want. Hope is being confident that no matter what happens in life, God will see you through. *"And we rejoice in the hope of the glory of God. Not only so, but we also rejoice in our sufferings, because we know that suffering produces perseverance; perseverance, character; and character, hope. And hope does not disappoint us.* (Romans 5:2b-5a)

Our circumstances can certainly disappoint us at times especially when we become too focused on ourselves. I believe God is challenging us to see our circumstances through His eyes.

While we are on earth, we will continue to face mountains but there are so many valuable lessons to learn during the challenging climb. I pray that you would gain godly perspective and endurance with every climb and that Jesus would be your source of hope.

The mountain of grief or despair may seem overwhelming. It may look impossible to climb. There appear to be too many obstacles in the way. You may think that there is no way up the mountain. You can't find the hope. You are too weak to climb; too weak to even crawl. The good news is that you can rely on God's strength. God will pick you up in His gentle yet strong arms and start carrying you up the mountain. He will carry you for as long as you need and as often as you need. And then one day you will be able to climb with the complete confidence that God will be right there with you to catch you when you fall. And I pray that God would put people on your path to support and encourage you along the way.

As you climb, believe that God loves you. Believe that God can make all things new. Believe that God wants to give you an abundant life but know that His definition of abundant is different from yours. Believe that God is more interested in your character than in your convenience. Believe that God can give you hope for a brighter future. Believe that nothing is impossible with God.

And then one day, after a lot of perseverance, you will reach the top of the mountain. There is joy at the top. There is peace at the top. There is hope at the top. But all those things are available and within reach throughout the entire journey. Unfortunately despair has a way of hiding them. It is true that these gifts are easiest to see at the top but I pray that joy, peace, and hope will surround you always. May God show you through His eyes that the difficulties you face can be transformed into a breathtaking mountain of hope.

Then you will know that I am the LORD; those who hope in me will not be disappointed. (Isaiah 49:23b). The marriage of Karen and Lee Dancey would seem like a fairy tale if I hadn't seen this blessed love story unfold before my very eyes. Karen's faith and the Lord's compassion and care for her and her young boys will encourage and bless many. As funeral directors, we minister to people during a very difficult and often tragic time in their life. Karen's story is a great reminder of the blessed restoration that is possible because of God's great love and compassion for His people.

Ann Randall Kendrick, Funeral Director at Pollock Randall Funeral Home in Port Huron, Michigan

ABOUT THE AUTHOR:

Karen Dancey lives in Southeast Michigan with her newly married husband, Lee, and their three precious sons. Back in 1994, Karen began a fun tradition of turning her annual Christmas letter into a poem; hence, her love for writing began. Since then, she certainly has had plenty of extreme life experiences to write about and she strives to keep focused on God through it all. In her spare time, Karen enjoys scrapbooking, walking with friends, and helping children read.

You are welcome to contact Karen at <u>karendancey@yahoo. com</u> to invite her to speak or to share your comments.

9 781449 716479